PROFITABLE POKER, by Hubert Phillips, is a volume for the reference shelf of every would-be Cincinnati Kid—which means just about anyone who plays, or has played, poker, whether the stakes are toothpicks or hundred-dollar bills. Phillips takes poker apart—both stud and draw—and puts it back together again. In between he's examined the origins of the game, its mechanics, an amazing variety of pots, poker psychology, the views of foreign and domestic experts, the mathematics of the game, and — certainly not least—how to win. A winner of a book, to be brief. •

—*ESCAPADE*

HUBERT PHILLIPS

Profitable Poker

ARC BOOKS, INC.
New York

Published by ARC BOOKS, Inc., New York, N.Y.,
by arrangement with Arco Publishing Company, Inc.
219 Park Avenue So., New York

Third Printing, 1970

Copyright © Hubert Phillips, 1960
Library of Congress Catalog Card Number: 66-12618
Printed in U.S.A.

In Memoriam

I.J.G.

('Can I play at your table?')

FOREWORD

The advice which I give embodies those principles of play which I have formulated over many years; reliance on them enables me to hold my own in any school of players known to me. And—as a perusal of the book will make evident—my views are fortified by the similar conclusions of three of my American friends, all recognised authorities on the game: Oswald Jacoby; Albert Morehead and John R. Crawford. I am most grateful to them all for allowing me to include excerpts from their books.

HUBERT PHILLIPS

TABLE OF CONTENTS

FOR AMARYLLA, PLAYING POKER
(1936)

Defiant your air, and yet a shade forsaken,
  And your eyes are laughing, although they seem to mock;
All of you laughed, when the last of your chips was taken:
  'There goes my new spring frock.'

And I think: she loves the game; she cannot forsake it;
  Excitement trembles yet on her feverish lips;
If I loved her, and gave my heart to her, she would stake it
  As readily as her chips.

Her eyes are blue; they are blue as the sun-kissed scilla;
  She loves me, I think; she loves me, she loves me not;
I would not lose my heart to you, Amarylla,
  For a thousand times the pot.
                              —from *Journey to Nowhere*

INTRODUCTORY

LET ME begin by quoting from *Culbertson's Card Games Complete*, by Albert H. Morehead and Geoffrey Mott-Smith. The authors describe in a few sentences how the game of Poker, as we now know it, originated:

' Poker is traditionally the national card game of the United States, but is known and played throughout the world and perhaps by more people than play any other card game. The modern game of Poker originated in the United States, probably in the early years of the nineteenth century; the first known reference to its present name is in the 1830s. Its origin, however, is ancient. The first game known to have been played on the same principles was a Persian game, As or As Nas; the principle of building structures — sequences, and cards of the same rank — was even more ancient in China, whence the game which we know as Mah Jongg, and our modern Rummy games. The development was gradual, through a long line of European and English games that included Pochen (bluff) in Germany — whence, no doubt, our name for the game. The American game crystallized as Straight Poker, the basic principles of which govern all Poker games, and branched off into two main families, Draw Poker and Stud Poker.'

There are several reasons for the increasing popularity of Poker:

(1) Poker is pre-eminently a social game. A full table consists of seven players, but it is a perfectly good game for five or six.

(2) Every deal is a separate event. One can join a table, if there is a vacancy, at any time, and quit at any time. Here, of course, I am referring to club Poker; one could hardly break up a table organized among friends merely because one happened to be losing, or because one had won so much that one felt impelled to go while the going was good.

(3) Every player is playing for himself alone. If he plays badly, therefore, no one is offended; indeed, since the game must be played for stakes (however trivial) the poor player won't encounter the black looks, and unkind comments, handed out to the duffer at Contract Bridge.

(4) The mechanics of the game are comparatively simple. One could, I suppose, learn in an hour or two how the simpler forms of the game are played. Here there is a sharp contrast to the mechanics of a game like Bridge, which it may take the beginner some time to master.

(5) But, while the mechanics of the game are simple, its technique takes a long time, and much practical experience, to acquire. Hence the Poker addict derives continuing pleasure from the exploration of the game's subtleties and from experimentation with its constantly-changing situations. To play Poker really well demands a combination of qualities which few of us can ever hope to possess. Patience; the capacity to concentrate; the capacity to think quickly; imagination; psychological insight; the indefinable quality called flair: all these play their part. One must keep one's temper, and one must not lose one's nerve, however adverse circumstances appear to be. As Barrie remarks in a different context: ' If courage goes, all goes.'

And these qualities — with which only one player in a hundred is endowed — must be reinforced by adequate technical equipment: a knowledge of the mathematical probabilities relevant to any given situation, and the capacity to deduce how the minds of other players are working. Every deal at Poker involves two quite different sets of decisions. ' Before the buy' one's decisions should be founded on considerations which are purely mathematical. To attempt to flout the laws of chance is a certain road to disaster. ' After the buy,' however, mathematics go by the board; psychological insight takes over. And the better psychologist will win.

Why Poker Must be Played for Stakes

Poker is unique among card games in that it must be played for stakes, however small. It cannot be played where there are no stakes, for the game resolves itself into competitive betting on the values of the hands which the various players hold, and the player who out bets his rivals may not have to show his hand. And obviously, if there were no stakes, every player could, with impunity, go on betting indefinitely, and there wouldn't be any game at all.

How large should the stakes be? Large enough for a player who plays recklessly to be restrained in his commitments; he must suffer in pocket, as well as in pride, if he spoils the game for other players by continually over-betting. But not so large that those who are participating must risk embarrassment. The problem which confronts any card club is to fix stakes which steer a middle course between the two extremes. The stakes should not be so high that they provide a means of livelihood for the quasi-professional. When this happens too many people will lose too much too quickly, and before long the game will collapse. I have seen this happen over and over again. But neither should the stakes be so low that those participating can treat them with contempt. Where this happens, there is no particular inducement to play the game well.

This is a counsel of perfection, of course, In every club there will be players to whom $5 — or $50 — means a great deal less than it does to others; they can afford to take greater risks, and, if the risks which they take are mathematically or psychologically defensible, they will have an advantage which must in time disrupt the game. Ideally every player should be just as unwilling to risk the loss of $5 as every other player. Such a situation isn't, in practice, likely to occur. But, all being well, it should be possible to establish a situation which affords enjoyment and mental stimulus to all those participating. The better players will always win in the long run; but they won't win so much that those with whom they play become too quickly discouraged to play with them.

A Family of Games

The next point to establish, in these introductory remarks, is that Poker isn't just one game, but a whole family of games. Moreover, new variations on its basic theme are continually emerging. *Culbertson's Card Games Complete* (English edition) lists over fifty different Poker games. I shall mainly confine myself in this book, to those which are well-established in our better-known card clubs. And — what is even more to the point — there is no generally accepted code of laws for any of the game's numerous variations. I give (in Appendix D) the laws in force at one of our better-known card clubs, but as every club has its own rules, it would be foolish to sit down to a game without first finding out in what respects they differ from those given here. Appendix B lists the ' Variations in Practice ' which it is important to find out about if one is playing in a club or ' school ' for the first time.

The Plan of this Book

To conclude these introductory comments, here is a synopsis of the contents of the book:

PART I

The play in each of these nine variations of the game is illustrated by a number of representative hands, in which emphasis is laid on the importance of understanding the relevant odds. Novices — or players who don't understand why a knowledge of these odds is important — should play these hands through, and should ask themselves how they themselves would play or bet in each of the situations presented.

PART II

By 'bluffery' I don't only mean bluffing; I mean the whole complex of circumstances which should decide when to bluff; when not to bluff; when to call a bet which appears to be a bluff; and so on.

A light-hearted but a useful chapter in which players of various types are presented, and some estimate made of how they are likely to fare in a club game.

Chapter XIV. Transatlantic Wisdom.

   Excerpts, with comments, from the writings of Oswald Jacoby, Albert Morehead, and John R. Crawford.

Chapter XV. Conclusion.

   A résumé of my own advice to club players.

APPENDICES

Appendix A. Glossary of terms used in Poker games.

Appendix B. Variations in club practice.

Appendix C. A brief note on Poker games not dealt with in this book.

Appendix D. Laws of Draw Poker.

Appendix E. Mathematical Data.

This explains, for the benefit of those who are interested, how the ranking of Poker hands is arrived at; how odds relevant to various situations are calculated; and so on. To many players such considerations will always rank among the Eleusinian mysteries; they couldn't care less how the odds (which they may or may not have learned) are calculated. But there are, I find, many others who, like me, are fascinated by the mathematics of Poker; and they will, I know, find this Appendix exciting.

PART I

CHAPTER I

THE POKER FAMILY OF GAMES
AND THEIR RELATIONSHIP
ONE TO ANOTHER

THOUGH they differ widely from one another, and though many of them seem bizarre, all Poker games resolve themselves into competitive betting on five cards. The best hand wins all the money that has been staked on that particular deal.

What is meant by 'the best hand'? It means *either* the hand which, when exposed, is seen to be superior to any of the hands competing with it, *or* a hand which is apparently such a good one that no other player is prepared to call the last bet made by the player holding it. When that happens the winning hand is not exposed; whether the winning hand was in fact superior to others is anybody's guess.

The Poker Family has two main branches. They are known respectively as Draw Poker and Stud Poker. In all games of Draw Poker five cards will have been dealt to each player before betting begins. In Stud Poker betting begins after each player has received only two or three cards.

Draw Poker

Draw Poker, in its turn, has two principal sub-families. These are (1) what is often called 'straight' Poker, in which a player who has once passed has no further interest in the deal; and (2) 'pots' of various types, in which any player can participate although he may have passed originally.

'Straight' Poker has two principal varieties. These are (a) what I call the 'Ante and Straddle' game, and (b) an

21

Ante and Straddle with a 'blind' opening bet by the player who is 'first to speak'. These terms will not be intelligible to readers who do not know the game already, but they will very shortly be explained.

Pots are of many different types. A 'pot' is a deal to which every player makes an agreed contribution before any cards are dealt at all. The 'pots' about which I shall have something to say are:

(1) *Jackpots*, which can only be opened by a player who has been dealt two Jacks or better.

(2) *Acepots*, which, similarly, can only be opened by a player who holds two Aces or better.

(3) *Freakpots*, for which there are no opening requirements. In a Freakpot, all the 2's are 'jokers': a 2 can represent any card in the pack. Indeed, it can represent a card which is not in the pack at all, for a player holding, say, all four Queens and a 2 can claim that his hand consists of five Queens.

In effect, Freakpots are played with a pack which differs radically from the pack used for pots of other types.

(4) *Misère Pots*. Here, again, there are no opening requirements. The pot is won by whatever hand would, at Straight Poker, be the worst one.

(5) *Choicepots*. This term covers a wide range of pots: a choice pot is so called because the conditions applicable to it depend on the whim of an individual. I shall only deal with one or two of the more familiar 'choices.'

Stud Poker

This is a more difficult game than Draw Poker: why this is so will, I hope, in due course be made clear. I propose to deal with three outstanding members of the Stud family:

(1) 'Short' or five-card Studs.

(2) Seven-card Studs.

(3) Seven-card Misère Studs.

The interrelations of the games listed above can now be shown diagrammatically. This diagram may help to bring home to the reader how extensive and far-reaching the ramifications of Poker are.

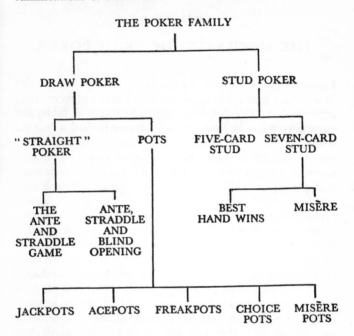

THE POKER FAMILY

DRAW POKER · STUD POKER

"STRAIGHT" POKER · POTS · FIVE-CARD STUD · SEVEN-CARD STUD

THE ANTE AND STRADDLE GAME · ANTE, STRADDLE AND BLIND OPENING · BEST HAND WINS · MISÈRE

JACKPOTS · ACEPOTS · FREAKPOTS · CHOICE POTS · MISÈRE POTS

This diagram is concerned only with the ten members of the Poker family of which I shall have something to say. There would be no point in including their numerous relatives (most of them of transatlantic provenance) since few of them have, so far, appeared here.

CHAPTER II

THE MECHANICS OF DRAW POKER

I SHALL assume, throughout this book, that we are playing in a club, where a full table consists of seven players. They are seated at a circular, or perhaps a heptagonal, table, and each player has in front of him a recess (called a 'bin')in which he places his chips. These chips are obtained from one of the club officials before the game begins. They are, in effect, a token currency. They will be of different colours, and perhaps of different shapes and sizes, and each chip will be marked with its notional value, e.g., $\frac{1}{2}$, 1, 2, 4, and higher values which may be 10, 20 or 25. The $\frac{1}{2}$, 1, 2, etc., represent the number of units that the chip is worth, and a unit may — in terms of cash — be anything from, say, sixpence upwards. Normally each player will start with chips representing 100 units in all — less whatever is deducted by the management by way of a 'cagnotte.' If a player is debited with the cost of 100 chips, and receives 98, he starts his game 2 chips to the bad. If a chip marked 1 represents one dollar, he is therefore paying $2 for the privilege of playing every time he sits down. Which means that only a good player, who never throws away more money than he can help, is likely to be in pocket at the end of, say, a year's play. For if he plays, say, ten times a week — and there are plenty of players who do — the fun of playing Poker will have cost him $1000 a year.

If a player has lost his 100 chips he can, of course, buy more. When he quits the table his account will be credited with the value of the chips that he returns.

A game will normally start as soon as five players have

expressed their intention of playing. They will draw for
seats, and must occupy the seats that they have drawn. The
numbering of the seats is clockwise, as shown in the
diagram. And throughout my illustrative examples I shall
make the player in No. 1 seat the dealer. I call him G; the
player to his left is A; then comes B, and so on. (*See diagram*).

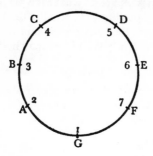

The game is played with a full pack of 52 cards, and
each deal, as I have mentioned, is a separate event. Each
player deals in turn: A follows G as dealer; B follows A;
and so on.

The Deal

The cards must be shuffled by the dealer, and they need
to be well shuffled. A perfunctory shuffle may not only produce distorted situations, but may allow a player of sufficient
acumen to draw deductions about the cards that other
players hold. After shuffling, the pack is presented for
cutting to the dealer's right-hand neighbour. The dealer
then proceeds to deal five cards, face downwards and one
at a time, to each player. When the deal is completed, the
players pick up their hands and examine them. They should
take care to hold their cards so that other players have no
opportunity of seeing them.

What happens next will, of course, depend on what type
of deal is in progress. We will consider them in turn.

(i) The Ante and Straddle Game

The player to the dealer's left (A) will have put one chip on the table in front of him. This is the Ante. The player next to the Ante (B) will have put two chips — the *Straddle* — in front of him. These are the only two players who need lose anything at all on the deal. Before we consider the play of this hand, let us ask ourselves what each player's objective is.

In brief, it is to produce, eventually, the best hand at the table. At this stage, then, let me explain the ranking of the various hands which a Poker player may hold.

RANKING OF POKER HANDS

This is a datum which every player should have at his finger-tips. In Ante and Straddle games, Jackpots, and Acepots hands rank as follows:

(1) Royal Straight Flushes.
(2) Straight Flushes.
(3) Four of a kind ('Fours').
(4) Full Houses.
(5) Flushes.
(6) Straights.
(7) Three of a kind ('Threes').
(8) Two Pairs.
(9) One Pair.
(10) Hands ranking lower than a Pair.

EXAMPLES (IN ORDER OF RANK) OF THE VARIOUS TYPES OF HANDS WHICH CAN BE HELD

(1) *Royal Straight Flushes*

A Royal Straight Flush (or Royal Flush) consists of the A K Q J 10 of any one of the four suits. In Poker, the Ace can be regarded as either the highest or the lowest card of its suit; here, of course, it is the highest card. It follows that only four different Royal Straight Flushes are possible. All suits rank equally; hence if two Royal Straight Flushes emerge in the course of one deal — the odds against this are astronomical — the two players holding them would divide the pot.

(2) *Straight Flushes*

A Straight Flush consists of five cards, all of the same suit and in sequence. Thus the following are Straight Flushes:

$$(a)\ \heartsuit\ K\,Q\,J\,10\,9$$
$$(b)\ \clubsuit\ 9\,8\,7\,6\,5$$
$$(c)\ \spadesuit\ 5\,4\,3\,2\,A$$

Should two Straight Flushes encounter one another in the 'showdown', the one that is headed by the higher card wins. (*a*) above would win against (*b*); (*b*) would win against (*c*).

(3) *Four of a Kind* ('*Fours*)

Here we have four cards of the same denomination, e.g.:

$$(a)\ 9\,9\,9\,9\,K$$
$$(b)\ 5\,5\,5\,5\,A$$

If Fours encounter one another, the higher denomination wins. Hand (*a*) beats hand (*b*).

In club play, any hand of these first three ranks normally carries a bonus (or penalty). The bonus is paid by each of the other players at the table, whether he has played in the pot or not. Bonuses are normally:

For a Royal Straight Flush ..	..	16 chips
„ Straight Flush ..	..	..	8 „
„ Four of a Kind ..	..	..	4 „

To qualify for a bonus, a hand does not have to win the pot. Thus if, in the showdown, one player produced a Straight Flush and the other Fours, and if there were seven players at the table, the former would collect 96 chips and the latter 24 chips. The player holding Fours collects his bonus even if he does not see his opponent's last bet.

In some clubs a 'bonus' hand is followed by a 'pot' in which the cards held, that qualified for the bonus, become 'wild' cards, i.e., jokers. Whoever gets one of these cards dealt to him can give it any designation he likes. Thus in the example just cited, where (say) $\diamondsuit$ 7 6 5 4 3 encountered K K K K 8, two 'penalty pots' would follow. In the first of these, the $\diamondsuit$ 7 6 5 4 3 would all be jokers; in the second, all four Kings.

(4) *Full Houses*

A Full House (or Full Hand) consists of three cards of one denomination and two of another. For example:

> (a) 9 9 9 2 2
> (b) 6 6 6 A A

If these two hands came into conflict, (a) would beat (b), because the three 9's are superior to the three 6's.

(5) *Flushes*

A Flush consists of five cards of the same suit which are not in sequence. Examples:

> (a) $\diamondsuit$ 10 6 4 3 2
> (b) $\spadesuit$ 9 8 4 3 2
> (c) $\clubsuit$ 9 7 6 5 3

In a showdown, hand (a) would win against hand (b), because it is headed by the higher card; hand (b) would beat hand (c). They are both headed by a 9, but (b) has the better next-highest card.

If all five cards in two competing Flushes are identical, their holders divide the pot.

(6) *Straights*

A Straight is five cards in sequence which are not all of the same suit. Examples:

> (a) $\spadesuit$ A $\diamondsuit$ K Q $\clubsuit$ J $\spadesuit$ 10
> (b) $\heartsuit$ K Q J 10 $\diamondsuit$ 9
> (c) $\heartsuit$ 5 4 $\clubsuit$ 3 2 $\diamondsuit$ A

Here (a) is a 'top Straight' or 'Straight to the Ace'.

(*b*) is a Straight to the King. (*c*) is the lowest-ranking of Straights, headed by the 5.

In a showdown (*a*) is superior to (*b*); (*b*) is superior to (*c*).

(7) *Three of a kind* ('*Threes*')

'Threes', as the name implies, consist of three cards of the same denomination and any two other cards which do not constitute a pair. If two such hands are in conflict with one another, the higher threes of course win. 9 9 9 6 2 beats 8 8 8 A K.

(8) *Two Pairs* (*or, as they are often called,* '*Two Pair*')

There are two cards of one denomination; two of a second denomination, and an odd one. If two such hands are in competition, the hand with the highest pair is the winning one; A A 2 2 5 beats K K Q Q J. If each hand is headed by similar pairs, the second pair decides the issue: A A 6 6 4 wins against A A 5 5 K. And, if both pairs are identical, the denomination of the fifth card decides the issue. J J 6 6 9 wins against J J 6 6 8. It can of course happen that all five cards are identical; the pot is then divided

(9) *One pair*

The holding of a Pair is very frequent; about 40 per cent. of the hands dealt at Poker contain one pair and three cards of other denominations. The higher pair wins when two such hands are in conflict: 6 6 5 3 2 wins against 5 5 A K Q If two hands contain identical pairs, the highest odd card settles the issue: 7 7 Q 3 2 wins against 7 7 J 10 9. The same principle applies if there are three, or four, identical cards: A A Q 6 2 wins against A A Q 5 4; K K 9 7 6 wins against K K 9 7 5. And (rare though it is) two hands may be identical throughout and divide the pot.

(10) *Hands below a Pair*

If hands are in competition which don't contain even one pair, the principles already presented apply:

A K 5 3 2 wins against A Q 10 9 8; A J 10 8 3 wins against A J 10 7 6. And so on . . . .

In *Freakpots* (where all four Twos are 'freaks' or jokers) the ranking of competitive hands is slightly different from that presented above. And in *Misère Pots*, where the 'worst hand' wins, it is altogether different. Freakpots are dealt with in Chapter VII, and Misère Pots in Chapter VIII.

If you have read the above explanations carefully, you should now have a clear idea of how Poker hands rank one against another. Their relative status depends upon the *a priori* chance of being dealt a hand of each type.

The number of Poker hands that can be dealt from a 52-card pack is 2,598,960. (This is based on the formula, known to everyone who has learned elementary algebra, $^{52}C_5$) The following table shows how many different hands, coming under each of the headings listed above, it is possible to deal:

(1)	Royal Straight Flushes	..		4
(2)	Other Straight Flushes	..		36
(3)	Fours ..	..	..	624
(4)	Full Houses	..	..	3,744
(5)	Flushes ..	..	..	5,108
(6)	Straights	..	..	10,200
(7)	Threes ..	..	..	54,912
(8)	Two Pairs	..	..	123,552
(9)	One Pair	..	..	1,098,240
(10)	No Pair..	..	..	1,302,540
		Total ..		2,598,960

There is no need to learn this table by heart. It is fascinating to players who are interested in mathematical theory; in Appendix E I show how each of its component figures is calculated. But a few very simple mathematical data are all that a Poker player needs. I shall return to this point presently.

We can now return to our point of departure (p. 26). We were considering an Ante and Straddle game. G has dealt the cards; A, the Ante, has compulsorily staked one chip; B, the Straddle, has compulsorily staked two. What happens now?

C — to the left of the Straddle — is 'first to speak.' He will look at his cards and decide whether he wants to play or not. If he does, he must stake 4 chips, and may stake as many as 8.* If he doesn't want to play, he throws his hand on the table face downwards, saying perhaps, 'No', and he then has no further interest in that deal.

D is the next player to speak. If C has thrown his hand in, D has the same options as were available to C: he can play for any number of chips from the minimum of 4 to the maximum of 8, or he can throw his hand in. If C is playing, D can either say, 'Play', and put in front of him that number of chips which is equivalent to C's, or he can raise C's stake by any number of chips not greater than double the number staked by C. Thus, if C has staked the minimum of 4 chips, D can say 'Play' and put 4 chips in front of him; or 'Make it Six', putting 6 chips in front of him; or 'Double', putting 8 chips in front of him. If C is playing for the maximum of 8 chips, D can play for any number of chips up to 16.

The initiative now passes to E, F and G in turn. If any of these first five players to speak — C, D, E, F, G — throws his hand in, the deal will have cost him nothing (unless it should happen that a player presently claims penalties for Fours or a Straight Flush). Now we come to the Ante (A). His options are the same as those available to the other players, but, if he throws his hand in, he loses the chip he has staked. And the Straddle, who is 'last to speak' is in the same position as the Ante. He must either play, increase the amount staked, or abandon his 2 chips.

If one of the players has increased the preliminary stake, by doubling or otherwise, he has initiated competitive

* As I have said already, there is no definitive code of laws for Poker, but this is, normally, the rule followed in most card clubs.

betting. Each of the players who has staked 4 or more chips originally has now to decide whether to accept the increased stake, to increase it further, or to abandon the chips he has put up. In private games, players will have made their own rules as to the extent to which any given stake can be raised. In most club games, 8 is the maximum number of chips by which another player's stake can be raised. This raising and re-raising of initial bets will continue until all the players are satisfied.

Examples of Betting Before the Buy

First Example. C, D, E, F, G have all thrown their hands in. A (the Ante) says 'Play' and increases his one chip to four. B (the Straddle) also says 'Play' and puts up two more chips. These are the only two players interested in the proceedings, and they have 8 chips in all to play for.

Second Example. C throws his hand in. So does D. E says 'Play', and puts up four chips. F throws in. G says, 'Double,' and puts up eight chips. A and B both throw in, abandoning their respective stakes. E accepts G's double, putting up 4 more chips. There are now these two players — E and G — left in the game, and they have 19 chips to play for ($1+2+8+8$).

Third Example. C throws his hand in. D says, 'Play,' and puts up 4 chips. E says, 'Double,' and puts up 8 chips. F throws his hand in. G says, 'Double again,' and puts up 16 chips. A throws in, abandoning his Ante; B says ,'Play,' and increases the two chips he has staked to 16. D says, 'Make it 24', and increases his stake from 4 to 24. E throws his hand in, losing his 8 chips. G says, 'And double again', putting another 16 chips in front of him. B raises his stake to 32; D reluctantly throws in. There are two players —G and B — left to contest the deal, and they have 97 chips in all to play for: 1 contributed by A, 32 by B, 24 by D, 8 by E, and 32 by G. Whichever of them wins the pot will have gained at least 65 chips; but, as we shall see, there may be more betting before the issue is finally determined.

To make the procedure crystal-clear, let me re-state these three examples in tabular form:

First Example:	C	D	E	F	G	A	B
Staked before the Deal:						I	2
Bets successively made:	No	No	No	No	No	4	4

There are so far 8 chips to play for, which must be won (together with such chips as are staked after the buy) by either A or B; or, possibly, they will divide the pot.

Second Example.	C	D	E	F	G	A	B
Staked before the Deal:						I	2
Bets successively made:	No	No	4	No	8	No	No
	–	–	8				

There are thus (so far) 19 chips to play for and two contestants, E and G.

Third Example.	C	D	E	F	G	A	B
Staked before the Deal:						I	2
Bets successively made:	No	4	8	No	16	No	16
	–	24	No	–	32		32
	–	No					

Hence there are (so far) 97 chips to play for, and, again, two contestants, G and B.

I have not complicated matters, in these preliminary examples, by indicating what cards those competing have in their hands. In this third example, we may take it that both G and B have exceptionally good hands: e.g., one of them might have been dealt a Flush, and the other a Full House.

Betting After the Buy

In every deal at Draw Poker there are two rounds of betting: the betting 'before the buy', which has been dealt with at some length, and the betting 'after the buy.' The latter, of course, only concerns the players who have not thrown their hands in.

As soon as the betting 'before the buy' is completed, the Dealer says, 'Cards?' or, 'How many?' Each of the players interested may now exchange as many of his cards as he likes for new ones. He must first throw his discards, face downwards, on to the table, and the same number of cards will be dealt to him, also face downwards. When this has been done, betting re-commences.

Examples of Betting After the Buy

We will consider how the betting, 'after the buy' might go in the three cases already presented.

First Example

The contestants (it will be recalled) are A and B, of whom A made the first bet. A says, 'Three cards'; he throws three and receives three. B says, 'One card' and, similarly, throws one and receives one.

Now it is up to A to bet first. He looks at his cards, says 'Double,' and puts 4 more chips in front of him. B throws his hand in. A collects the 12 chips on the table, of which 8 represent his own contribution.

Note.—A is not obliged to make a bet. He can (in some clubs) say 'Check,' which means that he is not raising the bet. In other clubs A must bet at least one chip, in which case he will probably say, 'Chip,' at the same time placing one more chip in front of him.

Very often a player will say 'check' or 'chip' before he has looked at the cards he has just received. In such cases it is customary in some clubs to say 'check dark' or 'chip dark,' as the case may be. The reason for this is that, in a good many clubs, the 'climate of opinion' is against a player's looking at his hand, finding that he has improved it, and then making only a small bet, or no bet, in the hope of getting a raise. And what I have called the 'climate of opinion' is a factor that a good player will take into account.

Second Example. E and G are contesting the pot; E has bet first, and G has doubled his bet. E now says, 'Three cards,' and checks before he has looked at them. G asks for one card, looks at it; and says ' Double,' putting up another 8 chips. E throws his hand in, and G, also throwing his hand in, collects the 27 chips on the table, of which he had himself contributed 16.

Third Example. G and B are contesting the pot, which has (so far) 97 chips in it. G (the dealer) has bet before B. He says, 'I'm playing these,' i.e. he is taking no cards. B also says, ' Playing these.' G now says, ' Double,' and puts another 8 chips. B says, ' See you,' also putting up 8 chips. Both players now expose their hands. G's hand wins against B's, and G collects the 113 chips on the table, of which 73 represent his profit on the deal.

It has taken me some time to explain the mechanics of the *Ante and Straddle game*. But if my explanation has been thoroughly understood, we are well on the way to understanding how Draw Poker is played. In a fast-moving club game, the average time taken to play a hand is rather less than a minute.

(2) The Ante and Straddle Game, with ' Blind ' Opening

This is a variation of the *Ante and Straddle game*, discussed above, which in some clubs has recently become popular. The best-equipped Poker players do not greatly care for it, for it militates against the dominance of that skill factor which makes the best players likely winners in Poker games. For it is highly probable that, in the course of an evening's play, one or other of the players who is not very expert will have more than his share of luck in his 'blind' openings, and will win money from most of the other players at the table. 'The result being,' I was told by a player who had access to his club's records, 'that, on balance, no one, however expert, is outstandingly successful.'

In other words, this is a variant of the *Ante and Straddle game* which reduces 'scientific' Poker almost to the level of a gamble.

The mechanics of this game can be simply explained in the light of what we know already. A puts up his Ante; B puts up his Straddle; and now C (who is first to speak) puts up a minimum of 4 chips before the cards are dealt. He may put up, if he likes, as many as 8 chips. This is the first bet made, and C, who makes it, is betting ' blind.'

As before, I will offer three examples of the betting 'before the buy' in this variation of the game.

First Example. Before the deal, A has put up one chip; B, two chips; C, four chips. The cards are dealt. C (first to speak) has already made his opening bet and cannot raise it. C has bet 'blind'; the other players will, of course, look at their cards. D throws his hand in; so does E. F says, 'Double,' and puts up 8 chips. G, A and B all throw their hands in. C, who has now looked at his cards, says, 'Double again,' and raises his stake to 16 chips. F throws his hand in. C collects the 27 chips on the table, of which 16 are his own, and the play of the hand is over.

Second Example. As before, A, B, and C put up one, two and four chips respectively before the cards are dealt. C has put up 4 chips; D says, 'Make it eight,' and puts up 8 chips. E and F throw their hands in. G says, 'Play,' and puts up 8 chips. A says, 'Double,' and puts 15 more chips in front of him. B and C throw their hands in; D contributes another 8 chips; so does G. There are now three players left to contest the pot: D, G and A, and, so far, there are 54 chips for them to play for.

Third Example. Before the deal, A puts up one chip; B puts up two; C, a gambler who is in winning vein, says, ' Play for eight,' and puts 8 chips in front of him. This is his opening bet. D, E, F, G and A all throw their hands in. B says, ' Make it 16,' and puts up another 14 chips. C, who has now looked at his cards, says, ' Make it 24,' putting up another 16 chips. B puts up another 8 chips. There are 49 chips in the pot, and C and B are left in to contest it.

I will re-state these manœuvres in tabular form:

First Example.	C	D	E	F	G	A	B
Staked before the Deal:	4					I	2
Bets successively made:	(4)	No	No	8	No	No	No
	16			No			

C collects 27 chips and the deal is over.

Second Example.	C	D	E	F	G	A	B
Staked before the Deal:	4					I	2
Bets successively made:	No	8	No	No	8	16	No
		16			16		

There are 54 chips in the pot, which D, G and A will contest. D will be first to speak after the buy.

Third Example.	C	D	E	F	G	A	B
Staked before the Deal:	8					I	2
Bets successively made:	(8)	No	No	No	No	No	16
	24						24

There are 49 chips for C and B to play for, and, after the buy, C will re-open the betting.

Betting After the Buy

This is on exactly the same lines as in the *Ante and Straddle game*. It is therefore unnecessary to give further examples of it here.

(3) Jackpots

With Jackpots, we embark on the investigation of Pots in the more restricted sense of the term. The five types of 'pot' of which I shall have something to say — Jackpots; Acepots; Freakpots; Choice Pots; Misère Pots — have this in common: that, instead of there being an Ante and Straddle, each player at the table contributes 2 chips to the 'pot' before the deal. There are thus, initially, 14 chips to play for. These 14 chips are placed in the centre of the table. Another feature which differentiates Pots from Ante and Straddle games is that whereas, in the latter, a player who has once passed is ' out,' a player who has passed in a Pot has the option of coming in after the Pot has been ' opened.' (American writers call the Ante and Straddle games 'pass and out' and Pots 'pass and back.').

In all Pots, the player to the dealer's left (A) is the ' first to speak.' He looks at his cards and says either 'Pass' or 'No' or ' Open.' The most he can open for is (normally) 4 chips, which he places in front of him. In the case of a Jackpot, he may not open unless he has been dealt a Pair of Knaves or better. If A passes, B in his turn passes or opens, and so on round the table to G, the dealer. If none of the seven players opens the pot, there must be a new deal and the Pot is refreshed or 'sweetened' by a contribution of (normally) a $\frac{1}{2}$-chip from each player. There will now, therefore, be $17\frac{1}{2}$ chips in the pot.

At this point, club practices diverge. At some clubs the deal passes from G to A, and B becomes first to speak. At others, the original dealer deals again. A second divergence of practice lies in the fact that, at some clubs, the number of chips required to open the pot is increased; at others, it remains at 4 chips. I shall assume, for the purpose of my illustrative examples, that the deal passes and that the opening requirement remains at 4 chips throughout.

Once the pot has been opened, each of the other players at the table has an opportunity of playing. He can either put up 4 chips, raise it to a maximum of 8 chips, or throw his hand in. If he has raised it to 8 chips, another player can raise the bet to 16, and thenceafter the amount staked can be raised 8 chips at a time. When everyone is satisfied, the betting 'before the buy' is over; cards will be dealt to players in accordance with their requirements, and betting 'after the buy' will begin. Here the first player to speak will be the opener of the pot, unless he has been driven out of it; in that case, it will be the first player to bet of those who are contesting the pot.

If the opener has been driven out of the pot, he retains his hand, placing his five cards face downwards in front of him. This is to enable him to 'show his openers' when the play of the hand is over. The penalties exacted for opening a Jackpot without having the necessary opening requirements vary from club to club.

Examples of Betting Before the Buy

First Example. A, B, C and D all pass. E opens the pot, putting 4 chips in front of him. F throws his hand in; G says, 'Play,' and puts up 4 chips. A throws his hand in; B plays, putting up his 4 chips. C and D throw in. There are thus 26 chips in the pot, and E, G and B will contest it after the buy.

Second Example. No one is prepared to open the pot. Each player adds to it a ½-chip 'sweetener' and the deal passes from G to A. Now B is first to speak. B passes after taking up the first three of his cards. C passes; D opens, putting 4 chips in front of him. E plays, putting up 4 chips. F doubles, putting up 8 chips. G throws in his hand. A plays for 8 chips. B now says, ' Make it sixteen,' and puts 16 chips in front of him. C throws in. D throws in, but lays his cards

face downwards in front of him, as in due course he must
show his openers. E throws in. F says, ' Make it 24,' and
puts up 16 more chips. A throws in. B puts up another 8
chips.

There are two players left in to contest the pot: B and F.
They are given cards, and F, who made a bet before B came
in, will be first to speak after the buy.

As before, I will now show in tabular form how the
betting went in these two examples.

First Example.	A	B	C	D	E	F	G
Chips contributed to the Pot:	2	2	2	2	2	2	2
Bets successively made:	No	No	No	No	4	No	4
	No	4	No	No			

There are thus 26 chips in the pot, to be contested by
E, G and B.

Second Example.	B	C	D	E	F	G	A
Chips contributed to the Pot:	$2\frac{1}{2}$	$2\frac{1}{2}$	$2\frac{1}{2}$	$2\frac{1}{2}$	$2\frac{1}{2}$	$2\frac{1}{2}$	$2\frac{1}{2}$
Bets successively made:	No	No	4	4	8	No	8
	16	No	No	No	24	No	No
	24						

There are $81\frac{1}{2}$ chips to play for ($17\frac{1}{2}$ in the pot, and 64
in front of the several players), and F and B will be given
cards by the dealer. F will be first to speak after the buy.

BETTING AFTER THE BUY

This will be on exactly the same lines as in the Ante and
Straddle games, and need not be exemplified here.

(4) Acepots

These are identical with Jackpots, save that the requirements for opening are stiffer: A Pair of Aces or better. Even

with seven players, an Acepot may be 'sweetened' several times before any player is prepared to open it. For this reason they have long been declining in popularity.

(5) Freakpots

These, too, are played in exactly the same way as Jackpots, but there are no opening requirements. I will say no more about them here, but the technical considerations which are applicable to them will be fully discussed in Chapter VII.

(6) Misère Pots

Misère (Worst Hand) Pots have, in recent years, become extremely popular. At some clubs, for example, there is a round of pots every ten minutes or quarter of an hour, and such a round may well consist of a Jackpot, a Freakpot, and two Misères. The reason why they command so much favour is that the player who is dealt a not very promising hand to begin with has a much better chance than he has in other pots of finishing with the winning hand. Why is this? Because a player who begins with, say, three Aces in a Jackpot cannot finish with a worse hand than the three Aces he started with, but a player who starts with a promising hand in a Misère Pot may well have it ruined if he buys even one card. Only a 'pat' hand — and a really good pat hand at that — can be bet with the near-certainty that it will win the pot.

The mechanics of a Misère Pot are similar to those of a Freakpot — i.e. there are no opening requirements — but there is one important difference. A player in a Freakpot can, if he likes, exchange four, or even five, of his cards for new ones. But a player in a Misère Pot cannot ask for more than three cards. This seems to be a generally followed procedure in club play.

In Misère hands the Ace ranks as the lowest card of its suit. Hence an unbeatable hand in these pots is 6 4 3 2 A, with at least two suits represented.

But a 'Royal Six' as this hand is often called, is of much more frequent occurrence than a Royal Flush. It has been shown (p. 30) that 2,598,960 different hands can be dealt from a pack of 52 cards. Only four of these are Royal Straight Flushes. But the number of 'Royals' that can be dealt in a Misère Pot is 1,020. (This is a very simple calculation from the mathematician's point of view. A 'Royal' consists of one card of each of five denominations. So the number that can be dealt is $4 \times 4 \times 4 \times 4 \times 4$, i.e. 1,024. Of these deals four are Flushes and a Flush can hardly win a Worst Hand Pot. $1,024 - 4 = 1,020$.)

I need say nothing more here about Misère Pots. In Chapter VIII I have dealt with the perplexing problem of how to play in them successfully.

(7) Choice Pots

Under this generic name are grouped the various 'fancy' pots that players are, on occasion, invited to nominate. In many club games Choice Pots are not introduced at all; in some others, a limited range of choices is permissible. In Chapter IX I deal briefly with one or two of the generally recognised variants.

To conclude this chapter, I should like to say something of the extent to which the well-equipped Poker player needs to concern himself with Mathematics. It should be evident, from what has been said already, that every hand dealt in a Draw Poker game resolves itself into two quite distinct components. Betting *before the buy* should (as subsequent chapters will show) depend upon a player's *a priori* chances of improving on the cards that he starts with. Unless, therefore, he has at least a rudimentary knowledge of the odds relevant to situations which constantly occur he is playing at a disadvantage. But betting *after the buy* is based upon quite different considerations, which may be roughly summed up as psychological.

But as it's the first part of the game, and not the second, that demands a modicum or mathematical knowledge, the player who hopes to win can't afford not to have it. On this point I should like to quote my friend Albert Morehead, who writes as follows in his fine book, *How to Play Winning Poker*:

'HOW FAR ARE MATHEMATICS IMPORTANT?

'You don't have to be a mathematician to be a good poker player. It doesn't even help.

'True, poker offers some of the most fascinating of mathematical problems, and for that reason has engaged the attention of the best mathematicians. Some of their researches invade the highest levels of the higher mathematics. Their findings are published in books. You can trust those books. I have read dozens of poker books and as far as I know Oswald Jacoby's is the only one written by a master mathematician, yet I have never seen a poker book in which the quoted odds are wrong by more than some insignificant fraction or percentage. *But you do have to have a knowledge of simple arithmetic, a memory for the simple odds that you read about in books, an understanding of what these odds mean, and a quick eye for appraising the size of the pot. It is considered neither cricket nor poker to stop and count the pot every time your turn comes and you have to make a decision.* (Italics mine).

'When you have the best hand around the table, and you know or feel sure that you have the best hand, mathematics doesn't enter into it at all. You simply shove your money into the pot. You may take some comfort from the figures, elaborately prepared by mathematicians, proving that the best hand going in is usually the best hand coming out; but what would it matter? Who ever heard of dropping the best hand?

'So the only mathematical questions arise when you may not have the best hand going in. In any such case, you must improve to win. You must then ask yourself three questions: (1) What are the odds against my improving? (2) What are the odds offered me by the pot? (3) What is the chance that I will win if I do improve?

'The first question is answered by tables of odds that you can quickly and easily commit to memory. . . . The second question — the odds offered by the pot — is a matter of an eyecheck of the pot or knowledge of how much is already in it and how much you have to put in. The third question — your chance of winning if you do improve — is answered partly by the table of probabilities and partly by your knowledge of the game.'

Oswald Jacoby (to whose mathematical knowledge Morehead justly pays tribute) effectively summarises in his book, *Poker*, what has already been said:

'To be a really good poker player it is essential to have a fair idea of the direct probabilities underlying various situations in poker in order to use them as a guide to one's general course of action. But one should always bear in mind that in the final bet or bets the psychology of one's opponents is much more important than any of the direct mathematical probabilities.'

The Odds That Every Poker Player Should Know

The table given on page 30 showing how the 2,598,960 different hands that can be dealt from a 52-card pack, is not there for the beginner to memorise. It is included (*a*) to show how the ranking of poker hands is arrived at, and (*b*) because it is interesting to those of us who are mathematically minded. What must be learned by heart (if one aims at holding one's own in the game) is a good deal less burdensome. Here are the data which, in my opinion, are essential.

(I) THE CHANCES OF BEING DEALT HANDS OF ANY PARTICULAR TYPE

A Full House	..	..	..	One chance in 700
A Flush ..	..	..	..	,, ,, ,, 500
A Straight	..	..	..	,, ,, ,, 250

Threes	..	..	..	,,	,,	,,	50
Two Pairs	..	..	..	,,	,,	,,	20
One Pair ..	..	..	..	,,	,,	,,	$2\frac{1}{2}$
No Pair ..	..	..	..	,,	,,	,,	2

(2) THE CHANCE THAT ANY OTHER PLAYER HAS
BEEN DEALT:

One Pair or better	..	..	One chance in	2
Two Pairs or better	..	..	,,	,,	,, 13
Threes or better ..	..	..	,,	,,	,, 33

(3) CHANCES OF IMPROVING HANDS
OF VARIOUS TYPES

A.— Drawing three cards to one Pair:

Odds against making Two Pairs or better	$2\frac{1}{2}$ to one
,, ,, ,, Aces Up or better	6 ,, ,,
,, ,, ,, Threes	8 ,, ,,
,, ,, ,, a Full House ..	100 ,, ,,
,, ,, ,, Fours	360 ,, ,,

But note that, if it is apparently essential that you should
make at least Aces Up, and you have in your hand one
Pair and an Ace, the Ace should be kept as a 'kicker.'
The odds against your making Aces Up or better are now
only 4 to one.

B.—Drawing two cards to Three of a kind
Odds against making a Full House
or better   ..   .. Nearly 9 to one
  ,,   ,,   ,,   Fours   .. $22\frac{1}{2}$,, ,,

C.—Odds against making a Full House where one holds Two Pairs:
$10\frac{3}{4}$ to one.

*D.— Odds against making a Flush where one holds four cards of
a suit:*   Nearly 4 to one (to be exact, 38 to 9).

E.—Odds against filling a double-ended Straight (e.g. where one
holds, say, 9 8 7 6): almost 5 to 1 (to be exact, 39 to 8).

It should not be a very exacting task for anyone of ordinary intelligence to memorise the simple data set out above. Yet I am constantly being asked what the odds are against improving a Pair to Threes, or against filling a Flush, by players who have been playing Poker for twenty or thirty years! I find this all but incredible.

Note: (a) The odds given above are in most cases approximate; but they are near enough for their divergence from the exact odds to be of no practical consequence.

(b) The odds which are relevant to Freakpots are, of course, completely different from those given above.

CHAPTER III

DRAW POKER:
THE ANTE AND STRADDLE GAME

In Chapter II, I have tried to make clear the mechanics of the various games which collectively constitute Draw Poker. In this and subsequent chapters I shall try to show how these games should be played.

First on the list stands 'straight' Poker, or what I have called the Ante and Straddle game. Here (it will be recalled) the player to the dealer's left (A) puts up a one-chip Ante; his left-hand neighbour (B) puts up, similarly, a two-chip Straddle. None of the other players has, at the outset, any chips at stake at all.

It follows that there is no sense in playing unless you have reason to believe that you are starting with what is probably the best hand of the seven that have been dealt. How are you to judge your prospects of success? The answer to this all-important question is derived from a table which is well worth studying, though it isn't necessary to try to learn it by heart.

The table shows how many chances you have of holding the best hand (before the buy) out of a total of 100 chances. Thus, with threes of a kind, the odds are 84 to 16 (five to one on) that you have the best hand dealt where you have six potential opponents. With better hands than this (a pat straight or flush, etc.), the odds in your favour are naturally even greater.

Again, holding Two Pairs originally, the odds that you hold the best hand dealt are 63 to 37 on (rather better than 3 to 2 on) against all the other players.

Clearly, then, you will — if you are 'first to speak'— play

CHANCES OF HOLDING THE BEST HAND
OF THOSE ORIGINALLY DEALT

YOUR HOLDING	NUMBER OF OPPONENTS					
	6	5	4	3	2	1
Three of a kind	84	87	89	92	94	97
Two Pair	63	68	74	80	86	93
Pair of Aces	49	55	62	70	79	89
,, ,, Kings	48	54	61	69	78	88
,, ,, Queens	32	38	46	56	68	83
,, ,, Knaves	25	32	40	50	63	79
,, ,, tens				44	58	76
,, ,, nines				39	53	73
,, ,, eights					49	70
,, ,, sevens					43	66
,, ,, sixes					40	63
,, ,, fives						60
,, ,, fours						57
,, ,, threes						53
,, ,, twos						50

on any hand which contains Two Pair or better. The need
to make critical decisions only arises when your holding is
no better than a Pair. With a Pair of Aces, you have 49
chances in 100 of holding a better hand, before the buy,
than any other player, i.e. you have an all-but-even money
chance. On a pair of Aces, then, C — the player first to speak
— should play; the fact that the Ante and Straddle are already
in the pot just tilts the scales in favour of his doing so.

But if C holds only a Pair of Kings, he will find that, in
the long run, it doesn't pay him to play. If, however, C has
thrown his hand in, the next player (D) is mathematically
justified in playing on a Pair of Kings. Similarly, where C
and D have thrown in, E is just about justified in playing on
a Pair of Queens; F, where C, D and E have thrown in, can
properly play on a Pair of Knaves — or, stretching a point
slightly— on a pair of tens; and so on. For G, who has only
two potential opponents, a pair of eights is good enough.

Let me repeat that the crucial question which each player
should ask himself is: Have I better-than-even chance of
holding, before any of us buys cards, the best hand at the

table? If the answer seems to be yes, I play; if not, I throw my hand in.

Hence we get a rule-of-thumb approach which (though he may, on occasion, see fit to deviate from it) should be so familiar to the tyro that he doesn't have to stop to think about it.

Here, then, is what I may call the beginner's guide to play in an Ante and Straddle game:

Position at the Table	No. of players still able to come in	Minimum requirements for playing
C	6	Pair of Aces
D	5	,, ,, Kings
E	4	,, ,, Queens
F	3	,, ,, Tens
G	2	,, ,, Eights
A (Ante)	1	An Ace and a King

A player who has only one potential opponent (i.e. the Ante) has a slightly better-than-even chance of starting better than the Straddle if he holds any pair at all. But an Ace and a King give a better chance of winning the hand (against one player) than does any low pair.

Ancillary to the above table is a second table which is equally well worth learning. This summarizes the minimum hands on which a player should come in when one bet of 4 chips has already been made. It is based upon an analysis of potential chances similar to that which has already been presented:

Where the first player is	It must be assumed his hand is not worse than:	And the next player to come in should hold at least:
C	A pair of Aces	Knaves up
D	,, ,, ,, Kings	Eights up
E	,, ,, ,, Queens	A pair of Aces
F	,, ,, ,, Tens	,, ,, ,, Aces
G	,, ,, ,, Eights	,, ,, ,, Queens
A	An Ace and a King	,, ,, ,, Sevens

Comments on the Above Directives

(*a*) This is about as far as we can go in the elaboration of hard-and-fast rules. If every player was completely *au fait* with the mathematics of Poker, and could be relied on to play, or refrain from playing, in accordance with mathematical expectation, it would be possible to formulate the principles on which a player should come in against two others; and so on indefinitely. Betting before the buy could then be determined automatically by an inspection of the seven hands dealt. But the psychological factors which make the game so interesting, outweigh mathematical considerations; one cannot even be certain that players who are in other respects well above the average will not, from time to time, deviate from the 'rule of thumb' principles indicated above.

(*b*) *Ante* versus *Straddle*. When the first five players have all thrown in, a special situation arises. The Ante will lose one chip if he does not play; he may therefore think it well worth while to take chances which a strict mathematical analysis does not justify. And, if he plays, a comparable problem is posed for the Straddle, who will forfeit two chips, when the Ante plays, unless he also plays or doubles.

In some schools it is accepted that the Ante may, if he wishes, ask the Straddle whether he (the Straddle) wishes to play. If the answer is ' No,' both players take back their chips. If this question is put to the Straddle, and he holds — or is purporting to hold — a good hand, he may, of course, elect to play for 8 chips. Now the Ante must either play for 8 chips or lose the chip he has staked.

(*c*) It may be thought by the tyro that this exhaustive consideration of the most profitable line of play, where there is only a chip or two at stake, is hardly worth bothering about. Anyone thinking so is very wide of the mark. If you are playing (as I often do) with 5s. or 10s. chips, to throw away half a dozen unnecessarily in the course of a single session may mean the unnecessary loss of some hundreds of pounds a year. No good player will let even one chip go without weighing the pros and cons of its sacrifice.

(*d*) There are two hands on which one should always play — provided the initial stake hasn't been doubled — regardless of the number of players participating. One of them is a pair of Aces. The odds (as we have seen, page 45) are only 5 to 2 against improvement, and Aces up will normally be good enough to win the pot.

(*e*) The other exceptional hand is a holding of four cards to a Straight Flush. Suppose, for example, that one holds the 9 8 7 6 of a suit. Either the 10 or the 5 of this suit will give one a Straight Flush (with its bonus of eight chips from each of the other players); any other card of the suit will give one a Flush; any other 10 or 5 will give one a Straight. Hence there are 9 cards of the suit, plus six other cards — 15 cards in all — which will give one what is probably a winning hand, so the odds are only 32 to 15 (just over 2 to 1) against success.

Illustrative Deals

FIRST EXAMPLE

The hands dealt are:

C: ♠ A 6 4 ♣ 5 3
D: ♠ K Q 2 ♡ J ♣ 7
E: ♡ 5 4 2 ◊ K 2
F: ♠ J ♡ Q ◊ J 9 6
G: ♣ A 10 8 6 ◊ 10
A: ♠ 5 ♡ K 10 ◊ 8 4
B: ♡ A 8 6 3 ♠ 3

Betting before the buy:

C throws in.
D throws in.
E throws in.
F with a pair of Knaves, plays, putting up 4 chips.

G has a pair of tens, which would not justify his playing against F, but he has also four cards to a Flush, headed by the Ace. The odds against his filling his Flush are, we know, just over 4 to 1, and, at the moment, he is only getting 7 to 4. Nevertheless, G (wrongly) decides to take a chance, and puts up his four chips.

A (the Ante) has a worthless hand, and throws in.

B (the Straddle) has 2 chips on the table already. Like G, he has four cards to a Flush, headed by the Ace. He is getting odds of 9 to 2 if he puts up two more chips, and is therefore fully justified in playing.

G (dealer) now asks the three players left in how many cards they require.

F: 'Three cards.' He keeps his pair of Knaves, throws the others, and receives from the dealer ◊ A 3, ♣ 2. He has not improved his hand.

G says, 'Dealer takes one.' He throws his ◊ 10 and receives ◊ 5.

B: 'One card.' He throws the ♠ 3 and receives the ♣ K.

Betting after the buy:

F: 'Check.'

G: 'Check.'

B: 'Double.' This, of course, is a bluff. B knows that F is not an adventurous player, and suspects that F has not improved. B puts four more chips on the table. F throws in. But G, who suspects that B is bluffing, puts up four more chips.

B's hand (A K 8 6 3) wins against G's (A 10 8 6 5) and B collects 21 chips, of which 13 represent his profit on the deal.

Tabular statement of the betting on this deal

	C	D	E	F	G	A	B
Staked before the deal	–	–	–	–	–	1	2
Betting before the buy:	No	No	No	4	4	No	4
Betting after the buy:				No	4	–	8
	–	–	–	–	8	–	–

F loses 4 chips; A loses 1; G loses 8; B wins 13.

SECOND EXAMPLE

The hands dealt are:

C: ♠ K 8 ♣ K ♡ 8 ◇ 2
D: ♠ A Q 2 ♡ J ♣ 7
E: ♡ 10 7 ◇ 10 ♣ 10 ♠ 9
F: ◇ 9 8 7 6 ♡ 9
G: ♠ 6 4 ♣ 5 3 ♡ 3
A: ♣ A 8 6 ◇ A 5
B: ♣ Q 9 4 ♠ 7 ◇ 3

Betting before the buy:

C: 'Play.' He has Kings up: a hand which, even without improvement, stands a fair chance of winning the pot. C puts up 4 chips. D throws in.

E: 'Play,' (putting up four chips). E would be justified in doubling on his three tens, and a good player would, I think, do so. His decision not to double — in the hope of winning more than he will win if he doubles — raises a question constantly debated: when is a hand 'too good to double on'? Most experts would agree that three tens doesn't come into this category.

F: 'Play,' (putting up four chips). F has four cards to a Straight Flush.

G throws in. Some players would take a chance on filling a Straight (6 5 4 3) but the pot at the moment only offers odds of 15 to 4, and the odds against

filling a Straight are just under 5 to 1. G's decision
is correct.

A: ' Play,' (putting up three more chips). A has a pair
of Aces, which — as has been said already — are
always worth playing on if the initial bet has not
been raised.

B throws in, abandoning his two chips.

There are thus, so far, 18 chips in the pot, and four
players — C, E, F, A — to contest the hand.

The dealer now gives cards.

C throws his ◇2 and receives the ◇ K. The odds are
43 to 4 (nearly 11 to 1) against his making a Full House,
but he has made a Full House, Kings high.

E throws his ♡ 7 and ♠ 9 and receives ◇ Q and ♣ J.
He has not improved on his original three tens.

F throws his ♡ 9 and receives the ◇ J. He has made a
Knave-high Flush.

A throws ♣ 8 6 and ◇ 5 and receives ♡ A 5 and ♠ 5.
He has made a Full House, Aces High. The odds against
his doing so are approximately 130 to 1.

The hands which are now in competition with one another:

C: K K K 8 8
E: 10 10 10 Q J
F: ◇ J 9 8 7 6
A: A A A 5 5

Betting after the buy

C checks before looking at the card he has just received.

E checks. A good player seldom doubles against a one-
card buy, and both C and F have drawn one card.
E still has hopes of winning the pot.

F doubles, putting up 4 more chips.

A doubles again, raising his stake to 16 chips.

C, after looking at his hand, makes the stake 24.

E throws in.

F throws in.

A doubles yet again, since it is long odds against C's holding either Fours or a Straight Flush.

C sees A and loses. A collects 78 chips, of which 46 represent his profit on the hand.

Tabular restatement of the betting:

	C	D	E	F	G	A	B
Staked before the deal:	–	–	–	–	–	1	2
Betting before the buy:	4	No	4	4	No	4	No
Betting after the buy:	(4)		(4)	8		16	
	24		No	No		32	
	32						

A's hand wins. He has won 46 chips. C loses 32 chips; E loses 4; F loses 8; B loses 2.

This deal—taken from actual play—shows more 'action' than one normally gets in an Ante and Straddle game. It's anyone's guess how high the betting would have been carried had F filled his Straight Flush.

CHAPTER IV

ANTE, STRADDLE AND COMPULSORY OPENING

I HAVE already remarked that this variant of 'Straight' Poker encourages the gambler. With a 'blind' opening, any fairly good hand may, if there are two or three gamblers at the table, be worth doubling on; more often than not (in my experience) one of the players makes the stake eight chips before the buy; if the opener, or any of the players sitting over the original doubler, has a really good hand, the stake will then be raised to sixteen chips; but also a speculative player may redouble a timid one when his cards don't, in fact, justify his taking the risk. Such tactics can't pay in the long run, but they may prove highly successful over a short period.

My own practice is to play a conservative game against gamblers, but to try to keep them guessing by making, from time to time, bets which are not theoretically justified. On the other hand, against conservative players one can take risks which are mathematically indefensible with some prospect of success. In short, this game isn't really Poker at all, but a bastard form of quasi-Poker for which it is difficult to formulate reliable principles.

Illustrative Deals

As before, A is the Ante and B is the Straddle. C, normally 'first to speak' has 'spoken' before the cards are dealt by putting up 4 (or perhaps more) chips in front of him before the cards are dealt. The player who has first to make a decision is therefore D, on C's left.

First Example

C has put up 4 chips. (It can't, in the long run, pay to put up more) G, the dealer, has dealt the following hands:

> D: ♣ K 9 6 ◇ 6 3
> E: ♠ 10 9 8 7 ♣ 5
> F: ♣ 10 7 ♡ 6 ♠ 5 ◇ 2
> G: ♣ A J 4 ♠ Q ♡ 5
> A: ◇ J 7 5 ♠ J ♡ Q
> B: ♠ A 6 ◇ K ♡ J ♣ 2
> C: ♡ 4 3 2 ♣ 3 ♠ 2

Betting before the buy

> D throws in.
>
> E (holding four cards to a Straight Flush): ' Play,' (puts up 4 chips).
>
> F throws in.
>
> G throws in.
>
> A (holding a pair of Knaves): ' Play,' (puts up 4 chips).
>
> B throws in.
>
> C has two small pairs. He cannot however double, even if he wished to do so, as he is already playing for 4 chips and none of the other players has doubled him.

The dealer now gives cards to C, E and A.

> C throws the ♡ 4 and receives the ◇ 10. He has not improved upon his two pairs.
>
> E throws the ♣ 5 and receives the ♠ 3. He has made a Flush, 10 high.
>
> A throws ♡ Q and ◇ 7 5 and receives ♡ K 8 and ◇ 8. He now has two pair, Knaves up.

Betting after the buy

> C (who has not yet taken up his card): ' Check.'
>
> E: ' Double,' (puts up another 4 chips).

A: ' I'll see the double.' (contributes 4 more chips).

C: ' No,' (throws in).

E's Flush wins, and he collects 22 chips, of which 14 represent his profit.

Tabular restatement:

	D	E	F	G	A	B	C
Chips staked before the deal:	–	–	–	–	1	2	4
Betting before the buy:	No	4	No	No	4	(No)	(4)
Betting after the buy:							(4)
		8			8		No

E wins 14 chips: 4 from C; 8 from A; 2 from B.

This was not a particularly interesting deal. A threw 8 chips away: to play on a pair of Knaves, when one player had played already, can't be justified; to see E's double was to throw good money after bad. A few elementary blunders of this kind can cost a good deal over a comparatively short period.

Now let me illustrate a more hectic episode, not untypical of this game as some clubs play it.

Second Example

C, who is in winning vein, has elected to play (blind) for 8 chips. The hands dealt are as follows:

D: ♠ K 6 ◇ K 3 ♡ 6
E: ♡ J 8 4 ♣ 8 2
F: ◇ Q 7 4 ♠ 7 ♣ 7
G: ♡ A 10 5 ♠ 3 2
A: ♠ Q 10 9 8 ◇ 8
B: ♠ 5 ♡ Q 3 ♣ 6 4
C: ◇ A 9 5 ♣ 10 3

Betting before the buy

D: ' Play,' (puts up 8 chips).

E throws in.

F: ' Make it 16.' (puts up 16 chips).
G throws in.
A: ' Play,' (puts up 16 chips).
B throws in.
C: ' Play,' (puts up another 8 chips).
D: ' Play,' (puts up another 8 chips).

The dealer now gives cards.

C asks for four cards, keeping his ◇ A. He receives
♠ A 4 ♣ A ◇ 10.
D throws his ◇ 3 and receives ◇ 6.
F throws ◇ Q 4 and receives ♡ 7 2.
A throws ◇ 8 and receives the ♠ J.

The hands now in competition are:

C: A A A 10 4
D: 6 6 6 K K
F: 7 7 7 7 2
A: ♠ Q J 10 9 8

— a Straight Flush; Fours; a Full House; three Aces.

This deal is one that actually occurred; it illustrates
how — once in a blue moon — an unlikely concatenation
of long shots can all come off. The odds against C's making
three Aces are approximately 60 to one; the odds against
D's Full House are 11 to 1; the odds against F's Fours are
45 to two; the odds against A's Straight Flush are 46 to one.
The odds against all four events occurring are therefore
about 800,000 to one!

Betting after the buy
C checks.
D raises the bet to 24 chips
F makes it 32 chips.
A makes it 40 chips.

Both C and D have sufficient sense to throw in. F, after
some hesitation, sees A, though he suspects that A has a

Straight Flush, since the latter did not double before the buy. A wins the pot, and both A and F collect penalties from the other players.

Restatement of betting in tabular form

	D	E	F	G	A	B	C
Chips staked before the deal:	–	–	–	–	1	2	8
Betting before the buy:	8	No	16	No	16	No	16
	16						
Betting after the buy:							(16)
	24		32		40		No
	No		40				

A wins the pot. He collects 82 chips from the other players, plus 8 chips from each (bonus for his Straight Flush). F collects 4 chips from each of the others (bonus for his Fours). So on balance A has won 106 chips. B has lost 14; C has lost 28; D has lost 36; E has lost 12; F has lost 4; G has lost 12.

CRITICISM OF THE PLAY

C, who opened unnecessarily for 8, wasted 4 chips by so doing and another 8 chips by playing for 16 when he had only one Ace to draw to. His comment that he was 'unlucky' to lose on three Aces shows that some players have strange ideas of what constitutes ' luck.'

D can't be faulted either for playing for 16 on Kings up, when he had already 8 chips in the pot, or for raising C's bet on his Full House. He played well in cutting his losses when the betting reached the 40-chip level.

F, had he been a master player, would not (in my judgment) have seen A's final bet. He does not have to be in at the finish to collect the bonus on his Fours. So our verdict is that 12 chips were thrown away by C and 8 chips by F, and that A profited by their mistakes to the tune of 20 chips.

CHAPTER V

JACKPOTS

JACKPOTS, it will be recalled, differ from the Ante and Straddle game in three important respects:

(i) Each player contributes to the 'pot,' the money being placed, before the deal, in the centre of the table. (In clubs, there is usually a circle marked out in the centre of the table. The contributions to the pot are placed therein, and the dealer is supposed to be responsible for seeing that everyone has subscribed to the pot before the deal begins.)

The contributions exacted vary from club to club. I shall assume, for the purposes of the analysis which follows, that the initial contribution from each player is 2 chips. There are thus 14 chips in the pot before the deal. In other clubs there may be a fixed amount which, in the course of a round of pots — seven deals if there is a full table — each player puts up in turn.

If a deal is passed out, the cards are re-dealt — in some clubs, by the same dealer; in others, by the player to his left — and the pot is refreshed or 'sweetened.' I shall assume that, in this event, each player contributes another $\frac{1}{2}$ chip to the pot; it would then, before the deal, be worth $17\frac{1}{2}$ chips.

(ii) No one can play till the pot has been 'opened.' And no player can open the pot unless the hand dealt to him contains a pair of Knaves or better. The opener may be driven out of the pot before the final bet is called, but in that case he will be called upon to show that he had 'openers.' The penalties for opening a pot where, in fact, the opener's hand lacks the necessary qualifications vary from one club to another.

(iii) A player who has passed before the pot has been opened is still entitled to play. (In American parlance, the Jackpot game is not 'pass and out' but 'pass and back.')

The player who speaks first is A, on the dealer's left. If A, B, C, D, E, F all pass, and G, the dealer, opens, A has now the opportunity of playing, as have each of the other players in turn.

Principles of Play

A player who has a pair of Jacks or better is not obliged to open the pot. Indeed, neither of the first two players to speak — A and B — should open the pot if he has only a pair of Jacks. Why not? Because this is to transgress the rule that one should not open a pot unless one has a hand which, theoretically, is likely to be the best hand at the table. And, with five or six players who have not yet spoken, a pair of Knaves is more likely than not to be inferior to one of the other players' hands.

This, I may say, is a perfectly sound principle which, in most clubs, is more honoured in the breach than in the observance.

It is perfectly permissible — so far as the rules of the game go — to pass on a really good hand (threes, or a pat straight) and take a chance that one of the other players will open. One can then double and, with luck, win a larger pot than would accrue had one opened it. But this manœuvre, technically known as ' sandbagging,' should be kept for 'tough' games; it is frowned upon in many clubs, and one loses more by ignoring their 'climate of opinion' than one is likely to gain by flouting it.

I shall assume, therefore, that we are playing a game in which 'sandbagging' plays no part; a player who has openers will open, unless he is first or second to speak and has nothing better than a pair of Knaves. On what principles should those who follow him (a) play, and (b) double?

A player who has a pair of Kings or better should, of course, enter the arena. With a pair of Knaves, or even a pair of Queens, a good player will think twice. It is almost certain that his hand is not as good as the opener's, and he is therefore competing at a disadvantage. The determining factor is the odds which the pot offers. If it has not been sweetened, there are 14 chips in it, and the opener's initial bet (4 chips) raises the amount to be won to 18 chips. One should not, therefore, put up 4 chips unless one's chances of winning against the opener are shorter than $4\frac{1}{2}$ to one.

Now if a player holds a pair, the odds against his finishing with a better hand than the opener's are theoretically 4 to one. (This is not a datum taken on trust; it is a complex calculation, but I have verified it for myself). If, therefore, one is last to speak and has any pair in one's hand, it is just worth while to compete in the pot. But, unless one is last to speak, it isn't worth while. For there are one or more players who still have a chance of coming in, and one's chance of winning the pot is *pro tanto* lessened. Hence a player who is sitting in B's seat is likely to be on a losing proposition if he comes in on a pair of Queens or Knaves where A has opened the pot, and it's longish odds against his winning if he comes in on a smaller pair.

In most of our clubs nearly every player enters a Jackpot on a pair. They are heartened by the fact that, every so often, their pair becomes threes and wins the pot. Admittedly they have one chance in nine of making threes, but what guarantee is there that the opener — or some other player — will not also produce threes or maybe a still better hand? I have often seen as many as four out of the six players who follow the opener play on a small pair. The fourth of them sees — if the opening bet has not been raised — that there are 30 chips to be played for. He is therefore being offered odds against his winning of 30 to 4, i.e., $7\frac{1}{2}$ to one. But he is now up against four competitors, and as likely as not his is the worst of the competing hands. He must inevitably lose heavily in the long run.

Moreover it is always possible — unless he is last to speak — that the opening bet will be doubled. Suppose that everyone comes in for the double. Now each of the players who started with a small pair can see that there 54 chips to be played for (40 + 14). The odds which it offers to each player who has put up 8 chips are 54 to 8, or less than seven to one. But, since we must assume that the doubler stands a better chance than the original opener of winning, the odds against the player with a small pair beating both of them are proportionately enhanced.

THE PROBLEM OF TWO PAIRS

Two-Pair hands constitute a real headache. I do not think I can improve on Albert Morehead's analysis of the problem:

'Some authorities have said that 90 per cent. of one's winnings or losses in poker can be attributed to the play of two low pairs (no higher than tens up). This is undoubtedly an exaggeration, but it serves to emphasise an important point.

'The basic principle governing the play of two pairs is this: Before the draw, the odds are nearly 2 to 1 on (in any draw game) that any two pair will be the highest hand. But the odds are 11 to one against improving.

'Mathematically, two low pairs have a better-than-average chance of standing up (without improvement) against one or two opponents; they stand to lose if three or more opponents are in the pot. Queens up is the lowest hand that stands to win against three opponents, and Aces up against four opponents. This takes into consideration the chance — one in twelve — of improving the two pairs you are dealt.

'From this knowledge has been derived a general rule that has amost become a poker precept: If you have two pair, raise at once, to drive out as many as possible of the other players.

'It is true that a raise tends to drive other players out and that you want other players driven out when you have two low pairs. Nevertheless, the rule is faulty. You should raise only when you are the second man (the one next to the opener.) You should merely stay when two players are in before you. You should drop two low pairs when there are three players in before you. When I say two low pairs, I mean in this case anything less than Queens up. I am also assuming that the pot is offering you no more than 6 to one. With two low pairs against three players, in a reasonably tight game, the odds are better than 2 to one that one of them will improve and beat you even if none of them has you beaten going in — and my experience is that one of them has you beaten going in, because there are simply not enough high pairs around to give each of three intelligent players a high pair that would justify his playing.

'Taking the other side of the medal, much money is lost by failure to back two pairs strongly enough against one or two other players who drew three cards. If you have created doubt in their minds by an occasional one-card draw of bluff, and if you have stayed after both are in, a one-card draw and a bet may get a call from a hand that did not improve . . .'

Morehead goes on to say that 'two low pairs should seldom be opened in a "pass and back in" game' (e.g., a Jackpot). 'The absence of high cards in the hand makes it more likely that another player will have a high pair and will open; and of all hands, two pair is the hand on which you want if possible to be the last to speak. Queens up or better may be opened, and should be opened if the over-head is high and the antes are worth grabbing, but many good players simply do not open on any two-pair hand under Aces up if they are earlier than fourth from the dealer.'

The advice given in this last paragraph does not, of course, apply to Jackpots played under the conditions I am postulating. Here the 14 chips which are in the pot before the deal make the odds one is getting for one's money sufficiently attractive to justify opening the pot on any holding of two pairs. Morehead is, I take it, visualising a Jackpot where the ante and straddle are put up in the ordinary way.

PLAYING ON FOUR CARDS TO AN OPEN-ENDED STRAIGHT

It is almost always worth while to play in a Jackpot on an open-ended Straight, as the odds against filling it are (as we know) just under 5 to 1; the only exception is where one is last to speak and no one else has come in against the opener. If three people, as well as the opener, are already in the pot, you have a 5 to one chance of filling your Straight, and the pot is offering you $7\frac{1}{2}$ to one. But if the pot has been doubled, your chances of success are less rosy. Suppose that A has opened the pot, that B has doubled (putting up 8 chips) and that D and E have come in for the double. You are F. You are now putting up 8 chips in the hope of winning 42 chips, or 46 if the opener stays for the double. To put up 8 chips in this situation isn't worth while. For one thing, either G or A may re-double; for another, it's quite possible that one of the players already in for 8 chips holds a better hand than that you can hope to make. Where there has been no doubling, it's reasonable to assume that, if you make your Straight, you will win the pot; but where there are three or four players willing to stay for a double that assumption becomes invalid.

If you have played for 4 chips on an open-ended Straight, and are subsequently doubled, the situation is again different. Suppose that A has opened the pot; that you, sitting in B's seat, elect to play; that the next four players throw in; and that G doubles. Suppose that A accepts the double. You have now the choice of abandoning your 4 chips, or of putting up 4 more. For those 4 chips the pot is now laying you the odds of over 9 to one, since your first 4 chips are already in the pot and cannot be retrieved. You should cheerfully stake the second 4 chips demanded.

But if you have come in for 4 chips and are doubled while there are still other players who have an opportunity of redoubling, you would — on a balance of considerations — be well advised to retire.

PLAYING ON FOUR CARDS TO A FLUSH

Here you are in a better position than a player who is drawing one card to an open-ended Straight. The odds against your succeeding are shorter, and you will finish (if you fill your Flush) with a better hand. So the advice given above is equally applicable.

WHEN SHOULD THE OPENING STAKE BE RAISED?

In my opinion you should double the opener when you are second to speak and hold two small pairs (i.e., pairs below Queens up); and you should double him, wherever you are seated, if you hold Aces up or better. If he, or another player, redoubles, you should not (in my opinion) double again unless you have three Aces or better.

Illustrative Deals

FIRST EXAMPLE

Each player has contributed 2 chips to the pot. A is first to speak.

The cards dealt are:

```
A: ♠ J 7  ♡ J  ◇ 7 3
B: ♠ 10 5 2  ♣ 10 8
C: ♡ Q 9 4  ◇ J 5
D: ♡ 8  ◇ K 9 2  ♣ K
E: ♠ A  ♣ 7 6 5 4
F: ♡ 7 6  ◇ 10 8  ♣ 2
G: ♡ A 10 3  ◇ 6  ♣ Q
```

Betting before the buy

> A opens the pot on his Knaves up, putting up 4 chips.
> B throws his hand in.
> C throws in.
> D plays on his pair of Kings, putting up 4 chips.
> E also plays on his open-ended Straight; he puts up 4 chips.
> F and G throw in.

There are thus three players contesting the pot.

Cards discarded and taken in

> A throws his ◇ 3 and receives ◇ Q.
> D throws ♡ 8 and ◇ 2 and receives ♠ K 9 and ♣ J.
> E throws his ♠ A and receives ♣ 3.

Hence the three hands contesting the pot are:

> A: J J 7 7 Q
> D: K K K J 9
> E: ♣ 7 6 5 4 3

Betting after the buy

> A checks.
> D doubles, putting up another 4 chips.
> E redoubles, putting up another 12 chips.
> A retires; D sees E's redouble and loses. E has won 34 chips.

Tabular re-statement

	A	B	C	D	E	F	G
Chips contributed before the deal:	2	2	2	2	2	2	2
Betting before the buy:	4	No	No	4	4	No	No
Betting after the buy:	(4)			8	16		
	No			16			

E has won 34 chips: 4 from A; 16 from D; 12 from the pot.

D played badly. He ignored the golden rule: 'Don't double against a one-card buy.' This rule, like every other, has its occasional exceptions; this situation isn't one of them. If D doubles and E has not improved his hand it's unlikely that he'll see D; he would only be justified in doing so if he started with Aces up, in which case he would almost certainly have doubled the opener. So D, in doubling, is on 'a hiding to nothing.'

SECOND EXAMPLE

The pot has been three times sweetened, so there are 24½ chips to play for before the deal.

The cards dealt are:

A: ◇ J 9 7 5 ♣ 10
B: ♠ A 8 7 ♡ 8 ♣ 8
C: ♠ J 5 ◇ 10 3 ♣ Q
D: ♡ K 4 ◇ K ♣ 7 6
E: ◇ A ♡ J 10 9 7
F: ♡ A 5 ◇ 6 2 ♣ A
G: ♠ K Q 10 ♡ Q ♣ 4

Betting before the buy:

A: 'No.'
B: 'I open.' B has three eights, which gives a good chance of winning the pot anyway.
C throws in.
D (a pair of Kings) plays (4 chips).
E plays. He is drawing to an 'inside' Straight Flush. The odds are 46 to one against his making his Straight Flush, but only 34 to 13 against his making a Flush or a Straight. (4 chips).
F plays on his pair of Aces (4 chips).
G plays. His play will be discussed below. (4 chips).
A plays on his four Diamonds.

So no fewer than six players are contesting the pot, and there are 48½ chips in it before the buy.

Cards discarded and taken in

A receives cards first, though he did not open the pot. He throws ♣ 10 and receives ♠ 6.

B, as often as not, draws only one card to threes. But, against five competitors, he thinks it better to go ' all out.' He throws ♠ A 7 and receives ♠ 3 and ♡ 3, which give him a Full House.

D throws ♡ 4 and ♣ 7 6, and receives ♠ 9 and ♣ 9 2.

E throws his ♢ A and receives ♢ 8 (giving him a Straight).

F throws ♡ 5 and ♢ 6 2, and receives ♠ 4 and ♣ J 5.

G — succumbing to a temptation which a good player resists — throws ♡ Q and ♣ 4, and draws two cards to his Royal Straight Flush. The odds against his making a Royal Straight Flush are 1,080 to one; they are also 1,080 against his making a Straight Flush, King high. The odds against his making either a Flush or a Straight are about 18 to one against him.

The cards which he receives are the ♠ 9 (O joy! O rapture!') and the ♡ 6 — which brings him down to earth with a bump.

The six hands now in competition are:

> B (opener): 8 8 8 3 3 (Full House)
> D: K K 9 9 2 (Kings up)
> E: ♡ J 10 9 ♢ 8 ♡ 7 (Straight)
> F: A A J 5 4 (Pair of Aces)
> G: K Q 10 9 6 (Kings high)
> A: J 9 7 6 5 (Knave high)

Betting after the buy

> B checks without looking at the card he has drawn.
> D checks.
> E doubles (puts up 4 more chips).
> F throws in.
> G throws in; so does A.
> B redoubles (puts up 12 more chips).

D throws in.

E sees B (putting up 8 more chips) and loses.

Tabular restatement

	A	B	C	D	E	F	G
Chips contributed before the deal:	$3\frac{1}{2}$	$3\frac{1}{2}$	$3\frac{1}{2}$	$3\frac{1}{2}$	$3\frac{1}{2}$	$3\frac{1}{2}$	$3\frac{1}{2}$
Betting before the buy:	No 4	4	No	4	4	4	4
Betting after the buy:	No	(4) 16		(4) No	8 16	No	No

So B has won $32+21$ chips: 53 chips in all.

G has thrown 4 chips away, and E has thrown away 12; he should neither have doubled B nor seen the latter's redouble.

CHAPTER VI

ACEPOTS

THIS will be a short chapter; Acepots have gone out of
fashion during the last thirty years, though they are still
played in some clubs. And most of what I have said about
Jackpots — e.g., the folly of playing on a small pair —
applies *a fortiori* to Acepots.

An Acepot differs from a Jackpot only in that the opener
must hold, not a pair of Jacks or better, but a pair of Aces
or better. From this there flow two consequences. (1) The
player who opens on the minimum — a pair of Aces — has
a much better chance of starting with the best hand at the
table than has the opener of a Jackpot who holds only a
pair of Jacks. (2) The pot may well be sweetened several
times before any player is able to open it.

For (1) the odds are approximately three to one against
a player who has only a pair of Jacks having the best hand
at the table initially; while the odds are three to two on a
player who has a pair of Aces only having the best hand.

And (2) it is roughly even money against any one of
seven players holding initially a pair of Aces or better.

If you are playing at a table where a round of Acepots
is from time to time part of the routine, you can hardly
lose if you play a conservative game and don't try to stage
ill-thought-out bluffs. For there will always be two or
three — perhaps more — players at the table who will try
their luck on a small pair, perhaps keeping a 'kicker' with
it; as in Jackpots, they will make two pairs or threes
occasionally, and will win the pot; and — since they don't
keep any sort of profit and loss account — will fail to

realise how many chips have been thrown away to offset these occasional successes.

The odds against a small pair beating the opener of a Jackpot are, we know, four to one. The odds against a small pair beating the opener of an Acepot are, roughly, $5\frac{1}{2}$ to one. If you are last to speak, and the pot, as it stands, lays you better odds than $5\frac{1}{2}$ to one, come in on your small pair. Otherwise, keep out. If even one player is in a position to raise you before the buy, your gamble isn't worth while.

On what hands, then, should you play in an Acepot? Answer: on a pair of Aces (never on a lower pair, save in the special circumstances detailed above); on two pairs; on four to an open-ended straight, if the pot lays you at least five to one; on four to a flush, if the pot lays you at least four to one.

If you have come into an Acepot on one of the above hands, and are doubled before the buy, should you accept the double? The answer here depends, again, on an assessment of the odds which the pot is offering. If you are last to speak after the double, and the money in the pot is now so considerable that you are still being offered attractive odds, stay. If that isn't the case, pack up.

Don't be influenced — as so many players are — by the notion that, as you have already put up four chips, that is a good reason for putting up some more. The money you have already put up belongs to the pot, and is no more 'your' money than it is anyone else's.

Finally: on what hands should one double the opener? Since the average winning hand in an Acepot is (theoretically) Knaves up, one should normally double on Queens up or better; the double on Queens up is more or less mandatory from the point of view of self-protection, just as the double on any two pairs is more or less mandatory in a Jackpot. If you are playing in a club in which 'sandbagging' is not frowned on, you may occasionally — if there are other players to come in after you — think it worth while to lie low on a really good hand, such as an Ace-high flush or a full house. But where — as in most cock-and-hen clubs — it is tacitly accepted that 'sandbagging' just isn't done, you will lose a lot more than you stand to gain by flouting public opinion.

An illustrative deal

G is, as usual, the dealer. The pot has already been sweetened four times, so, before the deal, it is worth 28 chips. Which means that, if the pot has been opened, a player putting up 4 chips to play is getting odds of eight to one.

These are the hands dealt:

A: ♠ K 8 ♡ K ◇ 8 4 (Kings up)
B: ♠ A 7 6 ♡ 8 ◇ 5 (four to an open-
    ended straight)
C: ◇ Q 7 3 ♡ J 2
D: ♡ 6 ◇ J 6 ♣ 8 6 (three 6's)
E: ◇ A 10 ♡ 10 3 ♣ 9 (pair of 10's)
F: ♣ K Q 4 3 ♠ 10 (four to a flush)
G: ♠ J ♡ 9 4 ♣ J 2 (pair of Knaves)

With 28 chips already in the kitty, keen betting before the buy can be expected. These were the bets actually made:

A: ' Open,' (puts up 4 chips).

B: ' Play,' (as I have just said, the pot is offering odds of 8 to one, and the odds against B's making what might well be the winning hand are only 5 to one).

C: ' No,' (throws in).

D: ' Play,' (bad judgment on D's part. It's long odds that he holds the best hand initially, but he should aim at discouraging competition).

E: ' Play.' (E's entry on a pair is not in accordance with the advice I have given. The odds against his improving are 5 to two; the pot is offering 10 to one; BUT there are still two players to speak. If either of them doubles, the bet may be redoubled by the time B has to speak next.)

F: ' Double,' (puts up 8 chips. (F is doubling on four cards to a flush. His double is a senseless piece of

bravado. If he is content to play, the pot is laying
11 to one, and the odds are only four to one against
his making his flush. By doubling, F is reducing the
odds which — at the moment — the pot offers from
11 to one to $5\frac{1}{2}$ to one.)

G: 'Play,' (G is gambling recklessly. He can't hope
to win unless he makes three J's, and the pot is only
offering $7\frac{1}{2}$ to one; the odds against G's making
threes are 8 to one.)

A: 'Play,' (puts up 4 more chips).

B: 'Play,' (another 4 chips).

D: 'Double,' (puts up 12 more chips).

E: 'No,' (throws in, very sensibly abandoning his
4 chips).

F: 'Play,' (8 more chips; but the pot is still offering
8 to one).

G: 'Play,' (throwing good money after bad).

A: 'Play.'

B: 'Play,' (He is staking 8 more chips, and the pot is
offering him 12 to one.)

There are now 112 chips to play for.

The buy

A throws $\diamond$ 4 and receives $\heartsuit$ 5. His hand: $\spadesuit$ K 8
$\spadesuit$ K 5 $\diamond$ 8 (Kings up)

B   ,, $\spadesuit$ A and receives $\spadesuit$ 9. His hand: $\spadesuit$ 9 7 6
$\heartsuit$ 8 $\diamond$ 5 (Straight)

D   ,, $\diamond$ J and $\clubsuit$ 8, and receives $\spadesuit$ Q 3. His hand:
$\heartsuit$ 6 $\diamond$ 6 $\clubsuit$ 6 $\spadesuit$ Q 3 (three 6's)

F   ,, $\spadesuit$ 10 and draws $\heartsuit$ 7. His hand: $\clubsuit$ K Q 4 3
$\heartsuit$ 7

G   ,, $\heartsuit$ 9 4 $\clubsuit$ 2; he receives $\clubsuit$ 10 $\spadesuit$ 5 2 (worthless). His hand: $\spadesuit$ J 5 2 $\clubsuit$ J 10

Only one player — B — has improved his hand. (The
a priori odds were roughly three to two against no player
improving. And the odds were roughly 12 to one against
B's being the one player who did improve.)

Betting after the buy

   A: 'Check.'

   B: 'Double,' (puts up another 8 chips).

   D: 'I'll see the double,' (8 chips).

   F: 'No,' (throws in).

   G: 'No,' (throws in).

   A: 'And I'll see the double.' (An idiotic decision. B may be bluffing, but it's a moral certainty that D has threes.)

The three players show their hands, and B collects a pot worth 136 chips.

Tabular restatement

	A	B	C	D	E	F	G	Total
Contributed before the deal:	4	4	4	4	4	4	4	28
Betting before the buy:	4	4	No	4	4	8	8	
	8	8		16	No	16	16	
	16	16						112
Betting after the buy:	(16)	24		24		No	No	
	24							136

B wins a pot worth 136 chips, of which 108 represent his profit.

COMMENT

There was a good deal of poorish play in this pot; I have tried to indicate where, in my judgment, those participating bet badly; and also to show how those who elect to play in these sizeable pots are lured on by the good odds which the pot offers. B was lucky to win, of course. An *a priori* chance of one in thirteen materialized: a not undeserved stroke of good fortune, as B played impeccably throughout.

A's play deserves consideration. Two pairs constitute a difficult hand to play (as has been pointed out in Chapter V). A's Kings up are slightly better than the average winning hand in an Acepot, but his bet was doubled and redoubled before the buy: this suggests that at least one of his opponents at least held threes or, at worst, Aces up. If he draws one card only, his only chance (11 to one against) is to make a full house. But if he throws his small pair and buys three cards, the odds are only 8 to one against his making three Kings. I should have been inclined to take this: the better of two slender chances of winning.

D, who started with three 6's, was unlucky, of course. Before the buy he had an odds-on *a priori* chance of winning. At this point (on the assumption that A is buying only one card) the chances, out of 100, that each player will eventually win are:

$$
\begin{array}{rr}
A: & 8 \\
B: & 13 \\
D: & 54 \\
E: & 18 \\
G: & 7 \\
\hline
 & 100 \\
\hline
\end{array}
$$

And the five players' several expectations of gain or loss (in chips) are:

$$
\begin{array}{ll}
D: +44 & A: -7 \\
F: +4 & B: -1 \\
 & G: -8 \\
\cline{1-1}\cline{2-2}
+48 & -16 \\
\hline
\end{array}
$$

The difference of 32 chips represents the original 28 chips in the pot plus 4 contributed by E.

CHAPTER VII

FREAKPOTS

A FREAKPOT offers a variety of Draw Poker which is quite different from any other. The 'freaks' are the four 2's, which are, in effect, Jokers: each of them can represent any other card. And in one type of hand — 'Fives' — a Freak can represent a non-existent card, since a hand consisting of, say, 8 8 8 8 2 can be declared as ' Five Eights.' What suit the Freak belongs to is anybody's guess!

It's obvious that, with four Jokers in the pack, every type of hand above the two-pair level can occur much more frequently in a Freakpot than in 'straight' poker, in Jackpots, or in Acepots. Below I repeat, for comparison, the distribu-

	Straight Poker	FREAKPOTS					
		NUMBER OF FREAKS					
		None	One	Two	Three	Four	Total
Royal Straight Flushes }	4	4	80	240	160	20	504
Fives	—	—	48	288	288	28	652
Straight Flushes }	36	32	576	2232	1232	—	4072
Fours	624	528	8448	19008	2832	—	30816
Full Houses	3744	3168	9504	—	—	—	12672
Flushes	5108	3132	7264	2808	—	—	13204
Straights	10200	9180	37232	19824	—	—	66236
Threes	54912	42240	253440	59376	—	—	355056
Two Pairs	123552	95040	—	—	—	—	95040
One Pair	1098240	760320	461728	—	—	—	1222048
No Pair	1302540	798660	—	—	—	—	798660
Total	2598960	1712304	778320	103776	4512	48	2598960

tion of the 2,598,960 hands that can ordinarily be dealt 'pat', and the corresponding number of hands of each type that can be dealt 'pat' in a Freakpot.

These figures are not, of course, intended for memorisation. They are merely included to show how much more frequent high hands — Fours or better — are in Freakpots than in straight Poker. The odds are only about 80 to one against one's being dealt such a hand ' pat,' whereas in straight Poker they are approximately 4,000 to one. And the number of hands susceptible of producing Fours or better if one buys only one card is, *pro rata*, equally impressive.

Principles of Play in Freakpots

As in Jackpots and Acepots, each player contributes 2 chips to the pot before the deal. A player can open on any hand, and can exchange as many cards as he likes. It is very unusual for a Freakpot not to be opened, for the odds against no player being dealt a Freak are about 113 to one.

The only hands on which one should open if one has not been dealt a Freak are (in my opinion) three Queens or better, and one should not open on less than three Aces or better if one is one of the first three players to speak. For it is more likely than not that someone else will open, and one can then decide what to do. If one holds, say, three Queens (with no Freak) and passes, and the pot is subsequently opened and doubled, it will generally pay to throw the hand in. If, however, one is one of the last three players to speak, and the pot has not been opened, one can open on any threes: there is a good chance that one will draw a Freak and so finish with Fours, or one may draw a natural pair, which would give one a natural Full House.

Hands containing one or more Freaks are in no sense inferior to 'natural' hands. Thus, if, in the showdown, one player holds K K K 8 5 and another holds K 2 2 9 3, the latter hand would win, because each player has three Kings but the next card—a 9—is superior to the other player's 8.

Hence, normally, no pot should be opened by a hand

which has no Freak in it. Some players will open on one Freak only, and nothing else of value in the hand, but this is not, in my judgment, sound policy if you are one of the first four players to speak. Holding one Freak, and nothing else of value, you should play in any pot which has been opened, and the more players there are in it the better, since this will probably mean that no one has more than one Freak.

You should always double the opener if you have two or more Freaks, and stay for any redouble. Similarly, you should play, holding two Freaks, in any pot doubled before the buy, and, again, stay if the pot is redoubled.

DISCARDING

Maurice Ellinger recommends keeping a Freak and an Ace, if that is what one holds, but here I don't agree with him. If you have come into a pot holding a Freak and an Ace, and you are only up against one or two other players, you should, I think, discard all one's cards except the Freak. This gives you the maximum chance of finishing with Fours or better.

BETTING AFTER THE BUY

Here it is almost impossible to formulate principles which should apply as a matter of course. Everything depends upon who the other players in the pot are, and what one knows about their style of play.

Illustrative Deals

FIRST EXAMPLE

The hands as dealt:

A: ♠ 9 6　♡ 10　♢ 8 7
B: ♡ Q 5 4　♢ Q　♣ Q
C: ♡ A 3　♣ A 9 5
D: ♠ 2　♢ 2　♡ 7　♣ J 4
E: ♡ 2　♠ K Q 10　♢ 3
F: ♠ J 7 5 3　♢ 6
G: ♢ A 10　♣ 8 7 6

Betting before the buy:

A (following my advice) does not open on his pat Straight.

B (also following my advice) passes on his three Queens.

C passes; he has only a pair of Aces.

D, with two Freaks, opens (4 chips).

E plays (4 chips).

F also plays (4 chips).

G throws his hand in.

A now doubles on his Straight (8 chips).

B throws in.

C throws in.

D refrains from redoubling. He may, after all, finish with nothing better than threes. He puts up 4 more chips.

E also puts up 4 more chips.

F (throwing good money after bad) likewise stays for the double and puts up 4 more chips.

Discards and cards drawn

A says, ' No cards,' since he has a 10-high Straight already.

D keeps only his two Freaks, and is given ♠ 8, ♡ 8 and ♣ 3. Hence he now has four 8's.

E decides to try to make his Royal Flush. This is, I think, a poor decision, for he should assume that all the Freaks have been dealt. If that is so, the odds against his making a Straight Flush are 45 to two; and, even if he makes one, it will not earn penalties from the other players. Penalties are only paid in a Freakpot on 'natural' Fours or Straight Flushes. E would therefore do better to draw four cards to his Freak. However, he throws his ◇ 3 and draws ♠ 4.

F keeps his four Spades. He shouldn't have been in the

pot in the first place, and should certainly not have
stayed for the double. He throws ◇ 6 and draws
♣ 10.

Betting after the buy

The hands in competition with one another are:

> D: Four eights.
> E: An Ace-high flush.
> F: A worthless hand (J high).
> A: A Straight to the 10.

D (who speaks first) doubles (16 chips). E sees him,
which is very foolish, since it's a near-certainty that D holds
Fours or better. F and A throw their hands in, and D wins
the pot.

Tabular restatement:

	A	B	C	D	E	F	G
Chips contributed before the deal:	2	2	2	2	2	2	2
Betting before the buy:	No	No	No	4	4	4	No
	8	No	No	8	8	8	
Betting after the buy:				16	16	No	
	No						

D wins 44 chips (32 + 12). E, F and A all threw money
away.

SECOND EXAMPLE

(A spectacular deal such as only occurs occasionally.)
There are, as before, 14 chips in the pot before the deal.
The hands as dealt:

> A: ♠ 10 6 ◇ J 5 ♣ 7
> B: ◇ A 7 4 ♣ A 3
> C: ♠ 9 8 7 ♡ 2 ♣ 2

D: ♡ J 8 5 4 ♣ 9
E: ♠ K 2 ◇ K 3 ♣ K
F: ◇ 10 9 8 2 ♣ Q
G: ♠ A J 4 ♡ 9 ♣ 5

Betting before the buy

A: 'No.'

B: 'No.'

C: ' Open,' (4 chips). C has a pat Straight Flush, J high.

D: 'No.'

E: ' Double,' (8 chips). He has four Kings.

F: ' Play,' (8 chips). He has four cards to a Straight Flush.

G: 'No.'

A now throws in.

B throws in.

C redoubles (puts in 12 more chips).

E doubles again (puts in another 16 chips).

F throws in.

C now makes it 32 chips, putting up 16 more

E puts up another 8 chips.

Cards asked for and received

C says, 'No cards'. (He is marked with either a Straight Flush or Fives.)

E says ' One card.' He throws the ◇ 3 and — a 46-to-one against chance—is given the ♡ K. Now he has five Kings, four of them 'natural' and therefore earning penalties.

Betting after the buy

C doubles (putting up 8 chips more).

E doubles again (16 more chips) and C sees him another 8 chips) and loses.

Tabular restatement

	A	B	C	D	E	F	G
Chips contributed before the deal:	2	2	2	2	2	2	2
Betting before the buy:	No	No	4	No	8	8	No
	No	No	16		24	No	
			32		32		
Betting after the buy			40		48		
			48				

E has won 92 chips (56 + 12 + 24 in penalties).

CHAPTER VIII

MISÈRE POTS

MISÈRE (Worst Hand) Pots have in recent years enormously increased in popularity, and in some clubs may be said almost to dominate the game.

The reason for their popularity isn't far to seek. In 'straight' Poker, Jackpots, etc., no one need finish with a worse hand than he started with.* But in a Misère Pot the most promising hand may — unless it's a 'pat' hand — be ruined in the draw, while a very large number of hands to which one, or two, or even three, cards are drawn may eventually win the pot.

> 'Hope springs eternal in the human breast;
> Man never is, but always to be, blest.'

A second reason for the popularity of Misère Pots lies in the endless complexity of the betting situations to which they give rise. They afford better opportunities for the exercise of judgment, subtlety and flair than do any other Draw Poker games.

The objective in these pots is, then, to finish with what is (or purports to be) the worst hand — judged by the standards of 'straight' poker — of those which are in competition. Since the Ace, in these pots, ranks as the lowest card of its suit, the worst hand that can be held is 6 4 3 2 A, where the five cards do not constitute a Flush. This hand —

---

* I say ' need ' advisedly, for a player starting with, say, the Ace of one suit and A K Q J of another will obviously throw the lone Ace and draw to his Royal Flush. He may thus have sacrificed a pair of Aces (or better) for an Ace-high hand.

6 4 3 2 A — is commonly known as a 'Royal Six' or a
' Royal.' It is however of much more frequent occurrence
than is a Royal Flush. Out of the 2,598,960 hands which
can be dealt 'pat', only 4 are Royal Flushes, but there are
as many as 1,020 'pat' Royals available. So that while you
can expect to get one Royal Flush in (approximately) one
deal out of 650,000, you can expect to get a pat Royal in a
Misère Pot in one deal out of 2,500.*

It might be interesting to carry the comparison farther,
and show how the best Misère hands that can be dealt pat
compare with their opposite numbers in 'Straight Poker'.

POSSIBLE POKER HANDS IN A 52-CARD PACK

In Straight Poker		In Misère Pots	
Royal Flushes:	4	'Royals' (6 4 3 2 A)	1,020
Straight Flushes:	36	Other 6-high hands:	4,080
Fours:	624	7-high hands:	12,240
Full Houses:	3,744	8-high hands:	34,680
Flushes:	5,108	9-high hands:	70,380
Total:	9,508	Total:	122,400

This means that whereas, in Straight Poker, you will be
dealt a Flush or better in about one deal out of 270, you
will—in a Misère Pot—be dealt a 9-high hand or better in
about one deal out of 20. This may well be a third reason
why Misère Pots are popular.

How Misère Pots are Played

The mechanics of Misère Pots follow the pattern with
which we should now be familiar. Each player (in the game
I am describing) contributes 2 chips to the pot; the
sweetener if the pot isn't opened (not at all a common
occurrence(is ½ chip).

A pot can be opened on any hand. *But no player may draw*

---

* In forty years or so I have only once been dealt a Royal Flush, and
  that, ironically, was in a Misère Pot, where it doesn't carry penalties.

more than three cards. This rule was, I daresay, introduced to protect foolish players against the consequences of excess folly, since one can hardly think of a more philanthropic gesture than drawing, say, four cards to an Ace in the hope of finishing with the best Misère hand. To draw three cards is quite silly enough.

ADVICE TO PLAYERS

Your position at the table is of the utmost importance. If you are first to speak you will need a really good hand to open on. In games where 'sandbagging' is frowned upon, many players are in the habit of 'passing blind' (i.e., without looking at their cards). This is obviously foolish. One player known to me abandoned this practice in a deal where, after he had passed blind, everyone else passed also. He then looked at his hand and found that he had been dealt a Royal. A practice which I often follow is to look at four of my cards; if I have a promising holding such as 7 4 2 A, I pass. I look at the fifth card after the pot has been opened.

But normally one will want to see all one's cards. One should play, first to speak, on any hand which is 8-high or better.

Unless it's a very poor 8 — e.g., 8 7 6 4 2 — it's more likely than not to win the pot. (The average winning hand is, in my experience, 8 7 5 x x). A hand which is 9-high is a more difficult proposition. It may well win the pot, and a really good 9-high hand (say 9 5 3 2 A) is worth opening on. Poor 9-high hands should be passed; one can always enter the pot later if one of the other six players has opened it.

The player who is second to speak is in a slightly better position, and each subsequent speaker can view his cards more optimistically if those before him have passed. After four passes, one would not only open on any 9-high hand; one might consider occasionally a good 10-high hand. You are dealt, say, 10 6 4 2 A. Four players have passed; you open. Against two or three other players you stand a good chance of winning by standing pat. But if one of the players who has passed doubles you, you can always throw your 10 and draw with excellent prospects to your 6 4 2 A.

Playing after the Pot has been opened

One should always play if one has a one-card draw to a good 8, or a respectable pat 9. On better hands (e.g., a good 8 pat) one should raise the opener, and normally, stay for a re-raise. Where a hand has been opened and doubled it is inadvisable to come in on a worse hand than a pat 7, while a pat 6 is worth another double.

But a great deal will depend, of course, on one's knowledge of the other players at the table. There is immense scope, in Misère Pots, for bluff and semi-bluff bids. To give just one example, suppose that a pot has been opened and doubled and that you hold 9 6 4 2 A. This is a hand that isn't normally likely to win a pot. But against two players who are playing a fairly free game there is something to be said for another double from you if you are the last player to receive cards. The opener of the pot (if he has accepted your re-raise) may have a pat 8, or he may hold 6 3 2 A and one high card. In the former case he will stand pat, in which case you draw. The second player may be similarly placed, and the same considerations apply. If both players draw one card and check, you stand pat and double again, and there's a good chance that both the other players will throw in.

Drawing cards

More often than not, a hand will necessitate the drawing of one card. A player who only played on pat hands in Misère pots would lose a great deal of money. You can expect to be dealt a pat 8 or better in about one deal out of 50. So you would contribute about 100 chips to fifty pots, plus whatever you staked when you did get your pat hand, in the hope of winning, at best, from 20 to 30. But if you draw one card to a good 8 or better, you will be playing in about one pot out of four, and can expect to win, roughly speaking, a third of them. Normally these transactions should show a small, but not inconsiderable, profit.

It's impossible to offer a more precise statement than the above, because (a) the relevant mathematics are extremely complicated, and in any case (b) are vitiated by imponderables which outweigh their importance; and because (c) much more depends on the psychology and style of play of those who are participating than on mathematical considerations. I have spent a great deal of time investigating the mathematics of Misère Pots, but only because they are (to a mathematician) fascinating in themselves. A knowledge of relevant odds is, of course, helpful; but, in itself, it doesn't get one very far.

Drawing two cards

These are not likely to win, as I shall hope to show in my illustrative deals and also in the analyses of typical situations with which this chapter closes. Nevertheless almost all players indulge in them far more frequently than is sensible.

Let me, on this point, cite two American authorities. First, Oswald Jacoby:

'Ninety per cent. of your play should be with pat hands or with hands where you need only a one-card draw. The two-card draw is a luxury that you should indulge in from time to time, but only on the following conditions:

1. Your three cards are 7 4 A or better, so that if you do make a perfect draw your hand will almost surely win the pot.
2. The pot has been opened and at least two other players have stayed.
3. You have reason to believe that there will be no raise before the draw.

'The probabilities of a two-card draw are as follows: drawing to 7 4 A your chance of making a 10-high or better is two in nine, of making a 9-high or better is one in seven, and of making an 8-high is one in eleven.'

These chances — given Jacoby's assumptions — just about justify drawing two cards to 7 4 A.

Albert Morehead dismisses the whole subject in one laconic sentence:

'One-card draws are common and are mathematically sound; two-card draws are almost as common and are almost never mathematically sound.'

Drawing three cards

Three-card draws in a Misère Pot are frequently encountered in most clubs. They fructify so seldom as to make them, from any standpoint, indefensible.

Three other Important Considerations

These are points not so far mentioned which every player should bear in mind:

(i) The number of players competing in a pot makes a lot of difference to the chances that the player who originally held the best hand will win it. If you start with, say, 8 7 4 2 A your prospects of winning against one player are excellent. But the outlook becomes less rosy with every added competitor. Whereas, in a Jackpot, you welcome competition where you start with, say, three Aces, you don't like to see other players queueing up against your pat 8 7. And if you have opened on, say, 6 4 2 A and one other card, there is not only the threat of several rivals, but the awareness which you should have that there won't be much of a selection of low cards in the seventeen from which you will draw one card to your ' Royal.'

(ii) The fact to which I have just drawn attention is frequently overlooked. Players are inclined to forget that if there are, say, six entrants in the pot they probably hold collectively twenty or even more of the 28 low cards in the pack (7's and under). Allowing for the fact that some at least of the few low cards available will duplicate your own, your chances of buying a card that you want are reduced almost to vanishing-point.

(iii) Don't overlook (as many players do) the danger of making a Flush or Straight when you buy one or two cards. 6 5 4 A is an attractive hand to buy to, but 6 5 4 2 isn't nearly so good: a 3 converts it into a Straight. And 6 5 4 3 isn't worth buying to at all if there are several competitors; a 7 or a 2 gives you a Straight; an 8 gives you a hand which is quite likely to be beaten; only an Ace keeps you in the picture. The *a priori* odds against drawing an Ace are 10¾ to one, but in a Misère Pot they are almost certain to be considerably longer. There may well not be an Ace available at all.

And, similarly, if you are drawing to four cards of the same suit, you must bear in mind that it's only 4 to one against your making a Flush.

Illustrative Deals

Each player has contributed 2 chips to the pot and G deals the following hands:

> A: ♠ Q 10 9 ♡ 5 ♣ 7
> B: ♠ 7 4 ♡ 10 6 ◇ 9
> C: ♡ K 8 ◇ 6 4 ♣ A
> D: ◇ K J 8 ♣ 5 2
> E: ♠ J ♡ J 9 3 ♣ 6
> F: ♠ 8 A ♡ 7 ♣ 4 3
> G: ♡ Q A ◇ Q 10 ♣ K

Betting before the buy

A: 'No.'

B: 'No.' His hand — 10 9 7 6 4 — might conceivably win the pot, but he decides (correctly) not to open 'under the guns' on so tenuous a holding.

C: 'Open' (puts up four chips). He proposes to draw one card to 8 6 4 A. Curiously I noticed, after framing these examples, that this opening is just good enough to avoid Jacoby's commendation. ' It is inadvisable,' he says, 'to open under the guns with worse than 8 6 4 2.'

D: 'Play' (4 chips). He will draw two cards to his
8 5 2. In my judgment this draw isn't worth while.

E: 'No' (throws in).

F: 'Play' (4 chips). F holds a pat 8 7 4 3 A. It would
be better play to double: he probably has the best
hand going in, but a one-card buy may well beat it
and he should aim at discouraging competition.

G: 'No' (throws in).

B: 'Play.' He will stand pat on his 10-high hand and
hope for the best.

There are now 30 chips in the pot (16 + 14) and four
players contesting it.

The buy: discards and cards drawn

G: ' Cards?'

B: ' No cards.'

C: ' One card.' He throws ♡ K and receives ♣ J.

D: ' Two cards.' He throws ◇ K J and receives ◇ 5 3.

F: ' Play these.'

The four hands in competition are:

> C (opener): J 8 6 4 A
> D: 5 5 8 3 2
> F: 8 7 4 3 A
> B: 10 9 7 6 4

Betting after the buy

C: 'Check.'

D: 'No' (throws in).

F: 'Double' (puts up another 4 chips).

B throws in.

C throws in.

F, who does not show his hand, collects the 34 chips in
the pot, of which 24 represent his profit.

Tabular restatement

	A	B	C	D	E	F	G
Contributed before the deal:	2	2	2	2	2	2	2
Betting before the buy:	No	No	4	4	No	4	No
		No	4				
Betting after the buy:			(4)	No		8	
		No	No				

SECOND EXAMPLE

This time we shall see what is infrequent, but by no means unlikely, three exceptionally good hands in conflict with one another. G deals these hands:

A: ♠ K 10 8 ♡ J ◇ J
B: ♠ 5 A ◇ K 2 ♣ 3
C: ♡ Q 10 ♣ K 9 8
D: ♠ 7 4 ◇ 5 A ♣ 2
E: ♡ 6 2 A ◇ Q 4
F: ♡ 9 8 ◇ 10 ♣ Q 6
G: ♠ 2 ◇ 8 3 ♣ 4 A

Betting before the buy

A: 'No.'

B: 'No.'

C: 'No.'

D: 'Open' (4 chips). He is opening on a pat 7 5 4 2 A, which is good enough to win perhaps 19 times out of 20.

E: 'Play' (4 chips). His four cards to a 'Royal' are good enough to double on.

F: 'No' (throws in).

G: 'Double' (8 chips). His hand — 8 4 3 2 A — fully justifies the double.

A: 'No' (throws in).

B: 'Play' (puts up 8 chips). He is playing on 5 3 2 A, and a 6 or 7 will give him a very good hand. A 4 will, of course, give him a straight, but B does not allow that possibility to deter him.

C: 'No' (throws in).

D: 'Play' (puts up 4 more chips). His hand is in fact worth a redouble.

E: 'Play' (puts up four more chips).

There are now 46 chips in the pot (32 + 14).

The buy: discards and cards received

B: 'One card.' He throws $\diamond$ K and receives $\spadesuit$ 6, which gives him 6 5 3 2 A: the next-best hand after a 'Royal.'

D: ' No cards.'

E: ' One card.' He throws $\diamond$ Q and receives $\spadesuit$ 3, giving him a ' Royal.'

G: ' I'm playing these.' He is standing pat on his 8 4 3 2 A. Had D elected to redouble, G would have thrown his 8, since his hand, as it stands would almost certainly not be good enough to win against two doubles.

The four hands in competition are:

> D (opener): 7 5 4 2 A
> E: 6 4 3 2 A
> G: 8 4 3 2 A
> B: 6 5 3 2 A

Betting after the buy

D (opener): 'Double' (raises his chips to 16).

E: 'Eight more' (raises his chips to 24).

G: 'No' (abandons his 8 chips).

B: 'Yet another eight' (raises his chips to 32).

D: 'No' (abandons his 16 chips. He has inferred— correctly — that he is up against at least one 6-high hand).

E: 'Make it 40.'

B: ' Make it 48.'

E: 'Make it 56.'

B: 'Very good: 56. I suppose you have a Royal?'

E: 'You couldn't be more right.' He shows his hand and collects the pot: 150 chips.

Tabular restatement

	A	B	C	D	E	F	G
Chips contributed before the deal:	2	2	2	2	2	2	2
Betting before the buy:	No	No	No	4	4	No	8
	No	8	No	8	8		
Betting after the buy:				16	24		No
		32		No	40		
		48			56		
		56					

E's pot is worth 150 chips, of which 92 represent his profit.

THIRD EXAMPLE

Hands dealt:

A: ♠ K 10 6 ♣ 3 ◇ A

B: ♠ 8 ♡ 6 5 A ◇ 3

C: ◇ K 3 ♣ 6 4 A

D: ♠ J 4 ♡ 7 2 ◇ 6

E: ♡ J 9 4 ♣ J 10

F: ♠ 9 ◇ 8 4 2 ♣ 7

G: ♠ Q ♡ K Q ◇ K Q

Note on the above hands

A can draw two cards to a Royal.

B has a good pat eight: 8 6 5 3 A. He has naturally high hopes of winning the pot.

C has four cards to a Royal: 6 4 3 A.

D's hand is not quite so promising as C's, but he has four cards to a seven: 7 6 4 2.

E's hand is obviously worthless.

F has a pat nine (and a very poor nine at that: 9 8 7 4 2.)

G has had the maddening experience (familiar to all players) of being dealt a pat Full House: K K K Q Q. Some players, dealt such a hand as this in a Misère Pot, go all out to win on it, 'just for the hell of it', and — if they drive their competitors out of the pot — will gleefully show what they played on. If you think indulgence in such antics is worth 40 or more chips, follow their example. Your popularity in your club won't suffer.

Betting before the buy

A: 'No.'

B: 'Open' (4 chips).

C: 'Double' (8 chips).

D: 'Play' (8 chips).

E throws in.

F: 'Double' (16 chips). He has made up his mind to attempt this semi-bluff if there are two players in before him.

G: 'No'; (But he can't resist the temptation to expose his hand, in the hope of eliciting a little sympathy. This should not, in fact, be done: no indication should be given during the play of the cards that have been dealt to anyone).

A: 'No' (throws in). A sensible decision. The two-card buy, with four other players in the pot, isn't worth 16 chips, and it may, of course, be re-raised by B, C or D.

B: 'Play' (puts up another 12 chips).

C: 'Play' (8 more chips).

D: 'Play' (8 more chips).

Things are going well from F's point of view. No one, apparently, has a good enough hand to raise again before the buy.

The buy: cards thrown and taken in

B (opener): asks for one card. He has decided that, with three players against him — one of whom has re-raised the pot—his pat 8 isn't good enough. A 4 or 2 will give him a 6-high hand. This shows that B isn't thinking clearly. Instead of taking — as he now is taking — a slender chance of winning, for which he has paid 12 chips, he should either have thrown in or stood by his 8-high hand.

As it is, he throws his ♠ 8 and receives the ◇ J.

C asks for one card. He throws ◇ K and receives ◇ 10.

D also asks for one card. In exchange for the ♠ J, he receives the ♣ 9.

F says: 'Playing these.'

The hands now in competition are:

> B: J 6 5 3 A
> C: 10 6 4 3 A
> D: 9 7 6 4 2
> F: 9 8 7 4 2

There are so far 78 chips to play for.

Betting after the buy

B (opener: 'Check'.

C: 'Check.'

D: 'Check.'

F: 'Double' (puts up 8 more chips).

B: 'No' (throws in).

C: 'See 24' (puts up 8 more chips). An observant player, he has seen F bring off his attempted coup already, and suspects that F may well be 10-high or even J-high.

D throws in, though in fact he holds the best hand, but he has come to the conclusion that either C or F will beat him.

F shows his hand and wins the pot. He has been saved by C's intervention.

Tabular restatement

	A	B	C	D	E	F	G
Contributed before the deal:	2	2	2	2	2	2	2
Betting before the buy:	No	4 16	8 16	8 16	No	16	No
Betting after the buy:		(16) No	(16) 24	(16) No		24	

F collects 94 chips, of which he has put up 26; a profit of 68 chips.

ADDENDA TO CHAPTER VIII

The studies reproduced here throw little light on the problem of playing Misère Pots successfully. I include them because I find such analyses quite fascinating, and I daresay they will prove equally fascinating to readers who are mathematically-minded. But if you are one of those Poker players who play by the light of nature, and are so allergic to arithmetic that you 'can't even add up the butcher's bill', pass on to the next chapter.

1. Mathematical Analysis of a Contest between Three Players

After the betting before the buy, there are three players left in a Misère Pot. The hands held by them are:

A (the opener): 8 6 5 3 2
B: Q 8 5 2 A. He will draw one card to 8 5 2 A.
C: J 9 6 3 A. He will draw two cards to 6 3 A.

Problem: What are their respective chances of winning?

First, let us tackle this problem in terms of the so-called *a priori* chances. These chances are calculated on the

assumption that each of the five cards not seen by a player
in his own hand is equally likely to be dealt to him when
he asks for cards. In a Misère Pot, as we have seen these
a priori assumptions are unrealistic: in a pot where there are
several players there isn't likely to be a fair proportion of
low cards available among the 17 which are left after all
the hands have been dealt.

However, let's pursue these *a priori* assumptions to their
logical conclusion.

(i) The odds against B beating A are 35 to 12, which
for our present purposes we will call 3 to one.

(ii) The odds against C beating A are 937 to 144, which
we can call 13 to 2.

(iii) If both B and C beat A, a more complex situation
arises. The odds that C will beat B on a hand which
is better than A's, where B has also beaten A, are
better than 2 to one.

Combining all these data, we need to conduct some complicated arithmetical operations, with the details of which
we need not trouble the reader. As a result, we find that,
out of 800 possible situations:

$$A \text{ wins outright } 520 \text{ times}$$
$$B \quad ,, \qquad ,, \qquad 173 \quad ,,$$
$$C \quad ,, \qquad ,, \qquad 80 \quad ,,$$
$$B \text{ and } C \text{ both}$$
$$\text{beat } A: \qquad 27 \quad ,,$$

In 20 of these 27 situations, C wins against B. So B
takes the pot 180 times, and C 100 times, out of 800.

Or, in terms of percentages, A wins 65 out of 100 times

$$B \quad ,, \quad 22\tfrac{1}{2} \,,, \quad ,, \quad 100 \quad ,,$$
$$C \quad ,, \quad 12\tfrac{1}{2} \,,, \quad ,, \quad 100 \quad ,,$$

Now let us assume that there are 38 chips in the pot. A
has bet 4 before the buy and another 4 after the buy, and
neither B nor C has raised him. The remaining 14 chips
were in the pot before the deal.

The test of a player's prospects of success or otherwise in a pot should be his a priori expectation vis-à-vis these 14 chips. If he expects (in the mathematical sense) that a particular play will, on balance, give him more than the 2 chips which he himself put in, he should play. Otherwise, he should not.

This I regard as an important principle. In Appendix C I give examples of its application.

Applying it here, we may say that A's 'expectation' is 65 per cent. of the 38 chips in the pot; that B's expectation is 22½ per cent. of them; that C's expectation is 12½ per cent. of them. So the division of the 38 chips should (in the long run) work out as follows:

A, who has put up 8 chips, expects to get 24·70:										+16·70
B, ,, ,, ,, ,, 8 ,, ,, ,, ,, 8·55:										+ 0·55
C, ,, ,, ,, ,, 8 ,, ,, ,, ,, 4·75:										− 3·25

The original 14 chips: +14·00

So B's play has been worth while; he stands to get back 55 of a chip towards the 2 chips he put in. C's play has not been worth while; he stands to lose 1·25 of a chip by entering the pot. A stands to win 13·45 of the 14 chips originally in the pot, plus 3·25 chips sacrificed by C.

All this is, of course highly theoretical and — let me emphasise once more — has next to no bearing on the play of a particular pot, where 'imponderables' are so much more important; yet — apart from its intrinsic interest — I have found these tenuous speculations helpful.

Now let me pass on the second point of interest; that, in a Misère Pot, *a priori* expectations are unrealistic because of the unlikelihood that there will be a fair share of low cards in the 17 cards remaining after the deal. This point could not be established mathematically in the present case without calculations so laborious that only an electronic brain could cope with them: it would be necessary to consider every relevant distribution of the first 35 cards among the several players, and then (in each case) to analyse the possibilities of the remaining 17! But I have made, at random, one assumption regarding the 17 cards that are left, and explored its relevance to the situation we are discussing. I assumed that the 17 cards were: K K Q Q J J 10 9 9 8 7 6 5 4 3 2 A. On this assumption, a series of arithmetical calculations shows that the respective chances of winning the pot (expressed as percentages) are:

A priori:

A: 77 per cent (65 per cent.)
B: 17 ,,   ,, (22½ ,,   ,,)
C: 6 ,,   ,, (12½ ,,   ,,)

This random sample shows A's prospects enhanced at the expense of both B's and C's, and I suspect that the percentages which it reveals are the more realistic of the two.

2. Mathematical Analysis of a Contest Between Four Players

In this exercise, I have assumed that there are four players contesting the pot, all on fairly promising hands.

A (the opener) holds 8 6 5 3 2
B is drawing one card to 8 5 2 A
C ,,   ,,   ,,   ,, ,, 7 6 4 2
D ,,   ,,   two cards ,, 6 3 A

How would you, having no further knowledge, assess the four players' relative chances of winning? Having posed the problem, I made this guess at the answer:

A's chance of winning   . .   50 per cent.
B's   ,,   ,,   ,,   . .   20 ,,   ,,
C's   ,,   ,,   ,,   . .   18 ,,   ,,
D's   ,,   ,,   ,,   . .   12 ,,   ,,

These percentages are based on the rule-of-thumb assumptions that the odds against B's beating A are roughly 3 to one; the odds against C's beating him, roughly 3 to one; and the odds against D's beating him, roughly 9 to 1.

How, if these assumptions are accepted as valid, does the allocation of the 14 chips originally contributed work out? We'll assume, as before, that A has bet four chips before the buy and four chips after the buy, and that no one has raised him. Then the long-run division of the 46 chips in the pot is as follows:

A, who has put up 8 chips, expects to get 23·0:   + 15·0
B,   ,,   ,,   ,,   ,,   8   ,,   ,,   ,,   ,,   9·2:   + 1·2
C,   ,,   ,,   ,,   ,,   8   ,,   ,,   ,,   ,,   8·3:   + 0·3
D,   ,,   ,,   ,,   ,,   8   ,,   ,,   ,,   ,,   5·5:   − 2·5
                                                    _____
                    The original 14 chips: + 14·0
                                                    _____

This hypothesis therefore justifies both B's entry into the pot and C's. A wins 12·5 of the chips in the pot, plus 2·5 chips which he wins from D.

Having completed this exercise, I embarked on one 'trial run,' assuming this time that the 17 cards still in the dealer's hands were:

K K Q J J 10 9 9 8 7 6 5 5 4 3 2 A

This particular assortment favours both C and D at the expense of B, for B needs to draw 6, 4 or 3; C, to draw 5, 3, or A; and D needs to draw two cards of the cards 7, 5 and 2 to beat all three of his competitors, while 8 5, 8 4, and 8 2 will beat A. C and D are favoured as against B because there are two 5's in the assortment available. Complicated arithmetical calculations produced the following percentage distribution of winning chances, those produced above by a rule-of-thumb hypothesis being given in brackets for comparison:

A's chance of winning   .. 50·8 per cent. (50 per cent.)
B's   ,,   ,,   ,,   .. 15·6 ,,   ,, (20 ,,   ,,)
C's   ,,   ,,   ,,   .. 17·6 ,,   ,, (18 ,,   ,,)
D's   ,,   ,,   ,,   .. 16·8 ,,   ,, (12 ,,   ,,)

C shows a minute profit on his participation in the pot; B and D show minute losses. This conclusion has no bearing on the play of this pot in practice, and is therefore of purely academic interest: every alternative assumption regarding the cards left in the dealer's hand would produce a different result. But it is interesting to discover that a random sample confirms with such exactitude our rule-of-thumb assumptions concerning A.

3. An Attempted Estimation (By Practical Experiment) of the Respective Chances of Players Drawing One, Two and Three Cards Respectively against a Pat Hand

This is not a mathematical exercise; it merely represents a little field-work in Cloud-Cuckoo-Land. In one of my clubs far too many players enter Misère Pots, for reasons which have already been discussed — to the great advantage in the long run of those who play a steady game. Quite often there are seven competitors for a pot, two-card buys being frequent, and three-card buys by no means uncommon where a pot is well supported. The occasional success of one of these bizarre ventures is so gratifying to those who embark on them that they dismiss without a moment's thought the heavy overheads incurred.

Hence I thought it worth while to experiment with a series of deals in which one player (A) is standing pat, while, of his six opponents, two are each drawing one card; two are drawing two cards; the other two are drawing three cards. In each case I gave the players the cards they would have received from the dealer; assumed there was no bluffing when it came to bet, and recorded which of the hands had won each pot. The results of 100 deals were recorded wherein A stood pat on a 7-high hand; 100 more where he stood pat on an 8-high hand; and so on up to a pat J-high hand (though experimentation here was hardly necessary). The tabulated results of the experiment are shown on next page.

TABULATED RESULTS OF 500 DEALS
WITH SEVEN CONTESTANTS

(The " Stock " of 17 cards re-shuffled each time)

THE PLAYERS' CARDS:

	A	B	C	D	E	F	G
Deals	76532	742A	863A	642	753	4A	65
1–50	40	4	—	1	3	1	1
51–100	45	2	—	2	—	—	1
Totals	85	6	—	3	3	1	2
	87532	742A	863A	642	753	4A	65
1–50	27	7	9	2	3	1	1
51–100	27	10	6	5	2	—	—
Totals	54	17	15	7	5	1	1
	98532	742A	863A	642	753	4A	65
1–50	21	9	13	2	3	1	1
51–100	20	12	10	4	2	2	—
Totals	41	21	23	6	5	3	1
	108532	742A	863A	642	753	4A	65
1–50	16	10	14	4	3	1	2
51–100	16	16	9	3	5	—	1
Totals	32	26	23	7	8	1	3
	J8532	742A	863A	642	753	4A	65
1–50	—	13	14	6	7	4	6
51–100	8	16	9	8	3	2	4
Totals	8	29	23	14	10	6	10
Totals 1–500	220	99	84	37	31	12	17

These results — for what they are worth — seem to me to confirm the generalised statements already offered in this chapter. On the basis of this far from adequate sample, it could be tentatively stated:

(1) That a player standing pat on a seven, against six opponents all drawing cards, has an odds-on chance of winning which is nearly six to one in his favour.

(2) That where he stands pat on an eight, he has a chance of winning which is slightly better than evens.

(3) That where he stands pat on a nine, the odds against him (with six opponents) are approximately two to one.

(4) That if he stands on a Knave, his chances of winning have almost disappeared. The odds which emerge here are more than eleven to one against him.

He would not do so well on his nine-high, ten-high and Knave-high hands had he fewer opponents. It is the multiplicity of compertitiors which reduces the chances of all of them.

Considering now the other players, we find that a player drawing one card to 7 4 2 A is — where there is so much opposition — encounters odds of four to one against his winning the pot. He must be getting much better odds than this. Suppose, for example, that all seven players are in the pot for eight chips, he is getting odds of nearly eight to one.

The player drawing one card to 8 6 3 A is here meeting adverse odds of about five to one. So he too is fully justified in playing.

Not so the two two-card buyers. The odds against them average about fourteen to one: nothing like good enough where the pot is offering less than eight to one.

As for the three-card buyers . . . . Let us draw a veil over their palpable ineptitude.

CHAPTER IX

CHOICEPOTS

A CHOICEPOT is a pot in the more limited sense of the term (i.e., every player contributes to the pot, and one can enter after an original pass) and that is all that can be said about it with certainty. As its name implies, it embodies the choice of whoever is the dealer, and the range within which that choice can be exercised may or may not be restricted. In some clubs Choicepots are never played; in some they are only played occasionally, and the dealer has only two or three options to choose from; in others, again, they are prominently featured. But the more extravagant types of Choicepot occur in privately organised games; I have taken part in many such games where every deal was a Choicepot, each player in turn giving rein to his imagination, and perhaps devising, with the general consent of the table, something altogether new.

Choicepots which are played occasionally, with a strictly limited range of options, include:

(1) Highest hand wins, all four cards of a nominated rank being Freaks; e.g., the four nines might be nominated. This hardly differs at all from an ordinary Freakpot, and I need say no more about it.

(2) Highest hand wins, but five nominated cards are Freaks; e.g., all the Spade honours, or the 8 7 6 5 4 of Diamonds. This is essentially a Freakpot, with one extra Freak.

(3) A Misère pot, but with four or five Freaks nominated as above.

(4) A Jackpot, Freakpot, or Misère Pot, to be won twice by the same player before its destination is settled.

Obviously such pots may involve those participating in a very considerable outlay, for the pot may (theoretically) involve no fewer than fifteen deals, of which none is passed out, before the final winner emerges; in such a case the odds offered by the pot to any participant, however large his holding, become so considerable that all normal rules of play go by the board.

I will shortly give examples of Pots of types (2), (3) and (4).

Other Choicepots which need only be mentioned cursorily include:

(5) Poker-pots, which are seldom played but actually afford a high test of skill. These are pots which resemble a Jackpot save that a player can open on anything.

(6) Pots to be divided between two hands: the best hand and the worst. This type of pot is very popular in America, but not so much in Draw Poker as in Stud Poker; American writers on the game have devoted much thought to the analysis of the High-Low form of Stud Poker. Its intricacies are of only academic interest here.

(7) Pots where each player is dealt, say, six cards instead of five. If he discards, say, three cards he can only draw two; if he discards only one he is standing pat on the other five. Obviously the hands in competition with one another will tend to be better than is normally the case.

(8) Pots in which an entire suit is nominated as Freaks. Such a Pot is a pure gamble: at least one player in a table of seven is fairly certain to finish with a Royal Straight Flush. So almost everything depends on the luck of the initial deal.

Illustrative Deals

FIRST EXAMPLE

A High Hand, in which the 6 5 4 3 2 of Clubs have been nominated as Freaks

The cards dealt are:

> A: ♠ J 7 4 ♡ A ◇ 6
> B: ♣ 4 (freak) ♡ K 5 ◇ 8 ♣ K

C: ♠ 6 2   ◇ J 10   ♣ J
D: ♡ 9 8 7 6 3
E: ♠ A 8   ♡ 10 4 2
F: ♣ 6 3 (freaks)   ◇ A   ♣ 10 8
G: ♣ 5 2 (freaks)   ♠ Q 9   ♡ Q

Betting before the buy

A: ' No.'

B: 'Open' (4 chips). B has three Kings: not a particularly good hand in a pot of this type. Since another
player would almost certainly open, he would have
done better to wait.

C: 'No' (throws in).

D: 'Play' (4 chips). A dubious decision on a Flush to
the 9, but D optimistically is planning to draw to
his open-ended Straight Flush. If the bet is raised
once or twice before the buy he will find himself
in a parlous position. One should hardly ever
play in these pots unless one holds at least one
Freak.

E: 'No' (throws in).

F: 'Double' (8 chips). F, with two Freaks, has three
Aces; also four cards to a Straight Flush.

G: 'Double' (16 chips). He holds four Queens, while
the possession of two Freaks ensures that, at most,
there will be three Freaks out against him.

Betting before the buy

A: 'No' (throws in).

B: 'Double again' (raises his stake to 24 chips). This
bet is a semi-bluff, designed to discourage competition.

D: (very foolishly) decides to stay, and puts up another
20 chips.

F: 'Play,' (puts up another 16 chips).

G: 'Make it 32,' (puts up another 16 chips).

B: ' Okay,' (another 8 chips).

D: 'Okay,' (the bit now firmly between his teeth).
F: 'And okay by me,' (another 8 chips).

There are thus four competitors, their holdings being:

    B: three Kings
    D: ◇ 9 8 7 6 (and the ♡ 3, which he will
       discard)
    F: three Aces
    G: four Queens

Cards discarded and received

B throws ♡ 5 and ◇ 8 and receives ◇ K 4. Now he
   has four Kings.

D throws ♡ 3 and receives ♡ J. He now has a worthless J-high Flush.

F throws ♣ 10 8 and receives ♠ 10 and ♣ 9. No
   improvement.

G throws ♠ 9 and is lucky enough to draw ♣ Q.
   (Five Queens).

Betting after the buy

B: 'Double,' (raises his stake to 40 chips).
D throws in.
F throws in.
G: 'Make it 48.'
B (suspecting that he is beaten): 'See 48.'
G shows his hand and wins the pot.

Tabular restatement

	A	B	C	D	E	F	G
Chips contributed before the deal:	2	2	2	2	2	2	2
Betting before the buy:	No	4	No	4	No	8	16
	No	24		24		24	32
		32		32		32	
Betting after the buy:		40		No		No	48
		48					

This is a not untypical five-freak pot. The best hand is very often Fours and B's four Kings would normally be good enough to win. G, who had the best hand going in (four Queens) was, of course, lucky to draw a fifth.

As it is, G collects a pot of 174 chips, of which 124 represent his profit. D and F had each thrown 28 chips away.

SECOND EXAMPLE

G has nominated as his 'choice' a Misère Pot in which the K Q J 10 9 of Hearts are Freaks

Such a pot as this is almost certain to be won by a 6-high hand, and it's by no means unlikely that the best hand will be a Royal. You have a better chance of being dealt a Royal pat in this pot than you have of being dealt a Straight in an ordinary hand.

No player should normally come into the pot without at least one Freak in his hand unless he has been dealt a pat Six.

Cards dealt

> A: ♠ K 8 7 ◇ J 9
> B: ♡ 8 6 ◇ 8 3 ♣ Q
> C: ♡ Q ♠ 6 5 ♣ 3 2
> D: ♡ 10 ♣ 9 6 4 ♡ A
> E: ◇ 6 ♠ 4 2 ♣ 10 A
> F: ◇ 7 5 ♠ 3 ◇ 2 A
> G: ♡ K 9 ◇ 10 6 ♠ A

Betting before the buy

- A: 'No.'
- B: 'No.'
- C: 'Open' (4 chips). He has 6 5 3 2 F, i.e., a 6-high hand.
- D: 'Double' (8 chips). D, with one Freak, has four cards to a Royal.
- E: 'No.' He also has four cards to a Royal, but the pot has already been opened and doubled. If he comes in, the betting (he thinks) may be carried

too far before the buy to make it worth his while
to play.

F: 'Play' (8 chips). A bad decision on a seven-high
hand.

G: 'Double' (16 chips). He has two Freaks, and is the
third of the seven players to have been dealt four
cards to a Royal.

A throws in.

B throws in.

C: 'Make it 24,' (puts up another 20 chips).

D: 'Play for 24,' (another 16 chips).

F: ' Play,' (another 16 chips). A moronic decision by
an inexperienced player.

G: ' Make it 32,' (puts up another 16 chips).

C: ' Very good,' (8 more chips).

D: 'Play,' (8 more chips).

F, having wasted 24 chips, reluctantly throws in.

There are already 134 chips in the pot.

Cards thrown and received

C: 'Play these.'

D throws ♣ 9 and draws ♡ 3, giving him a Royal.

G throws ◇ 10 and draws ♡ 5, which gives him
6 5 3 2 A — a hand identical with C's.

Betting after the buy

C: 'Check.'

D: 'Check' (!) He is confidently expecting a double
from G, who is, he knows, inclined to bet
recklessly.

G: ' Make it 40,' (puts up another 8 chips).

C: ' I'll see 40," (another 8 chips).

D: ' Make it 48,' (another 16 chips).

G: ' Seeing 48,' (another 8 chips).

C: ' And I'm seeing 48,' (another 8 chips).

D shows his hand, and wins a pot worth 182 chips.

Tabular restatement	A	B	C	D	E	F	G
Chips contributed before the deal:	2	2	2	2	2	2	2
Betting before the buy:	No	No	4	8	No	8	16
	No	No	24	24		24	32
			32	32		No	
Betting after the buy:			(32)	(32)			40
			40	48			48
			48				

Of the 182 chips collected by D, 130 represent his profit.

NOTE ON THE ODDS LAID BY THE POT
AT SUCCESSIVE STAGES OF THE BETTING

I have already mentioned (page 105) that one of the factors which should determine whether to play in a pot, or to stay in it, is the odds which the pot lays compared with the odds against improving one's hand. This deal affords an excellent opportunity of illustrating the point. The table below, ancillary to my 'Tabular restatement,' shows what odds the pot was offering to those who participated at each stage in the betting. It will be seen that, on promising hands, comparatively short odds were accepted in the early stages of the betting in the confident expectation that they would ultimately lengthen.

Chips in the pot before the deal: 14. Successive amounts staked by C, D, F and G; successive values of the pot; and the odds offered by the pot at each stage of the betting.

	C	D	F	G
Betting before the buy:	4 (14)	8 (18)	8 (26)	16 (34)
Odds:	$3\frac{1}{2}$: 1	$2\frac{1}{4}$: 1	$3\frac{1}{4}$: 1	$2\frac{1}{8}$: 1
	20 (50)	16 (70)	16 (86)	16 (102)
Odds:	$2\frac{1}{2}$: 1	$4\frac{3}{8}$: 1	$5\frac{3}{8}$: 1	$6\frac{3}{8}$: 1
	8 (118)	8 (126)		
Odds:	$14\frac{3}{4}$: 1	$15\frac{3}{4}$: 1		

	C	D	F	G
Betting after the buy:	Check	Check	—	8 (134)
			Odds:	16¾ : 1
	8 (142)	16 (150)		8 (166)
Odds:	17¾ : 1	9⅜ : 1		20¾ : 1
	8 (174)			
Odds:	21¾ : 1			

THIRD EXAMPLE

The Dealer has nominated a Misère Pot, to be won by the same player twice.

Such a prize as this pot will be is bound to produce much more liberal betting than in an ordinary pot. Any promising two-card buy is likely to be made, and three-card buys will be by no means infrequent, since any player who has won the pot once will take every opportunity of bringing off his second win before a rival does so.

I will not bore the reader by offering — what would not be particularly illuminating — a detailed account of the betting before and after the buy on the successive hands played in this pot, but will content myself with a résumé of what occurred, plus a tabular statement showing how the money mounts up. This (like the rest of my illustrative hands) is based on my recollection of what took place in a pot actually played.

First deal. A, B, E and F contested the pot. A opened it. F (playing on a pat nine-high hand) doubled the opener before the buy; A (with four cards to a six-high hand) did not redouble; B and E stayed. A made a 7-high hand; he re-doubled; F saw him and lost. There were now 62 chips in the pot, and A had one match in front of him indicating that he was a winner.

Second deal. The deal had passed to A. Everyone contested the pot. E opened, holding four cards to a 7-high hand. F and G came in; A, who had a pat eight, doubled. The next five players all stayed for 8. G doubled on four cards to

a six; A doubled; E stayed; G doubled again and A and E
both played for 32. Before the buy there were 190 chips in
the pot. E made his seven-high hand; but G did better still
and made his six-high hand. E doubled after the buy; G
doubled again; A threw in; E saw G and lost. The value of
the pot was now 224 chips, and A and G were half-way
towards the final goal.

With so many chips to play for, the pot had now become
a ' free for all,' and it is not worth while to give details of
the bets made before D, overhauling three competitors, won
the fifth pot played for. Six players competed in two of these
deals, and all seven in the last of them. Here D—who had
just scraped home in Round Four—dealt himself 6 5 3 2 A
and bet this fine hand to the best advantage.

Tabular Summary of the Betting

	Chips in the Pot							Progressive Total
	A	B	C	D	E	F	G	
Contributed before the first deal:	2	2	2	2	2	2	2	14
First deal: Betting before the buy:	4	4	No	No	4	8	No	34
	8	8			8			46
Betting after the buy:	16	No			No	16		62
	Winner of this deal: A							
Second deal: Betting before the buy:		No	No	No	4	4	4	74
	8	8	8	8	8	8	16	126
	24	No	No	No	24	No	32	174
	32				32			190
Betting after the buy:					40		48	214
	No				48			222
	Winner of this deal: G							

	A	B	C	D	E	F	G	*Progressive Total*
Third deal: Total
Nos. of chips bet:	8	64	16	–	64	48	40	462

Winner of this deal: E

	A	B	C	D	E	F	G	
Fourth deal: Total
Nos. of chips bet:	32	–	40	40	24	40	16	654

Winner of this deal: D

	A	B	C	D	E	F	G	
Fifth round:	80	16	8	80	80	24	64	1,006

Winner of this deal, and of the pot: D

D was thus fortunate enough to win a pot worth over 1,000 chips (the equivalent of about 30 ordinary Misère Pots) in what had developed into very nearly a pure gamble. No fewer than 352 chips were staked in the fifth deal because of the desperate efforts of A, D and G — each of whom was half-way home — to prevent D's scoring his second win. His final raise (from 72 chips to 80) was seen by A on a good nine and by D (with more justification) on a good seven. G, taking a more realistic view, had retired holding a poorish seven-high hand.

D, the winner of this pot, had only put 128 chips into it: barely one-eighth of its total value. He had played cautiously until the fourth deal, staying out of two deals altogether, and only risking 8 chips in another one. This is sound play: the hard-headed player won't vary his normally restrained game until the pot begins to lay odds which justify taking risks that aren't normally worth while. When D made his final bet (8 chips) he was getting odds of over 120 to one against a hand that was a virtually certain winner.

His competitors — tending to plunge heavily when they had each won the pot once — tended to overbet their hands. E lost 224 chips; A and G each lost 168. B and C had played with commendable restraint. F threw a good many chips away.

One moral which emerges from this illustrative deal is the unsuitability of a pot that needs to be won twice where the maximum permissible bet is 8 chips. It produces situations where the player who has comparatively restricted resources is in a relatively weak position. Some different scale of permissible bets should be prescribed — e.g., a maximum bet which is related more realistically to the rapidly-increasing value of the pot.

CHAPTER X

SHORT (OR FIVE-CARD) STUD POKER

All Stud Poker games are essentially different from Draw Poker games, in that betting begins when only two (or maybe three) cards have been dealt, and another round of betting follows the dealing of each additional card. Hence, with each successive round of betting, one has more information at one's disposal about the cards which other players hold; and, since any player may at any time retire, at the same time 'folding' his cards (i.e., placing them face downwards in front of him), one has little hope of winning unless one has memorized the cards that have been exposed. Or, at any rate, the cards which are relevant to one's own hopes of improvement.

Hence the skill factor in Stud Poker games is higher than in Draw Poker games: unobservant players, and players who can't concentrate, are almost certain to lose their money.

The Mechanics of Five-Card Stud

In a club game, each player will, initially, place (say) one chip in front of him. This is all that he need lose.

The dealer now gives each player one card, dealt face downwards, and then another card, face upwards. The player inspects the card dealt to him face downwards, then lays it down again, face, downwards in front of him. There follows the *first round of betting*. The player who bets first is he who has the highest exposed card; if two players have equally high cards, the first to bet is the one nearest to the dealer.

Now another card is dealt, face upwards, to the players

who are still in the game, and the *second round of betting* follows.

After this, every player still in the game receives a fourth card, face upwards; then comes the *third round of betting*.

If there are still two or more players left in the game, they are now dealt their fifth, and last, cards. These, again, are dealt face upwards. The *fourth (and final) round of betting* concludes the proceedings.

Illustrative Deals

I will assume that we are playing in a club game where the initial stake is one chip from each player. I will also assume that betting is regulated by rules which would be imposed in many of our clubs: that, until the final round, no player may bet more than one chip, or raise a bet already made by more than one chip; and that, during the first three betting rounds, the total raise may not be more than four chips. After the final deal, however, the player to speak first may bet four chips, and his bet may be raised and re-raised in the usual way. Checking is allowed throughout.

FIRST EXAMPLE

Each player has put up one chip. G (dealer) deals these cards:

	Exposed	*Hole Card*
A:	♥ 9	♣ 9
B:	♣ 6	♥ 7
C:	♠ 4	♠ 5
D:	♠ A	◇ K
E:	♥ 5	◇ 4
F:	◇ Q	♠ 2
G:	◇ 3	◇ 10

First Betting Round

D (with an Ace exposed) speaks first.

D. 'Make it two chips.'

E: 'No' (turns his exposed card face downwards).

F: 'Two chips.'

G: 'Two chips.'

A: 'Make it three chips.'

B: 'No' (turns his exposed card face downwards).

C: 'Three chips.'

D: 'Three chips.'

F: 'No' (abandons his two chips).

G: 'Three chips.'

Another card is now dealt to each of the four players still in the game. The cards now are:

	Exposed		Hole Card
A:	♣ A ♡ 9		♣ 9
C:	♠ 7 4		♠ 5
D:	♠ A ♡ K		◇ K
G:	♡ 10 ◇ 3		◇ 10

Three of the four players are encouraged by the outcome of this deal. C has three cards towards a Straight Flush; D has a pair of Kings; G has a pair of Tens.

D is still first to speak: his A K is better than A's A 9.

Second Betting Round

D: 'Check.'

G: 'Make it four chips.'

A: 'Four chips.'

C: 'Four chips.'

D: 'Four chips.'

(In American games, where betting is likely to be on a much more liberal basis than that postulated here, there would by now, almost certainly, be a great many chips to play for. C and D might well bet competitively, and so drive A and G out of the pot.)

Now for the penultimate deal. At the end of it the cards in the four hands are:

	Exposed	Hole Card
A:	♣ A ♡ 9 ◇ 6	♣ 9
C:	♠ 7 6 ♡ 4	♠ 5
D:	♠ A ♡ K ♣ 4	◇ K
G:	♡ 10 ◇ 3 ♠ 3	◇ 10

Now it is for G to speak first, since he has a pair of 3's showing.

Third Betting Round

    G: 'Make it five chips.'

    A: 'Five chips.'

    C: 'Five chips.'

    D: 'Five chips.'

Cautious play on the part of A, C and D — since it's fairly obvious that G has two Pairs.

The fifth (and last) cards are now dealt to the four competitors:

	Exposed	Hole Card
A:	♣ A ♡ 9 ◇ 9 6	♣ 9
C:	♠ 7 4 ♡ 6 ♣ 3	♠ 5
D:	♠ A ♡ K ◇ 8 ♣ 4	◇ K
G:	♡ J 10 ♠ 3 ◇ 3	◇ 10

A has made three Nines and C has made a Straight. Now it's up to A to open the betting.

Fourth (and last) Betting Round

    A: 'Check.'

    C: 'Check.'

    D: 'Check.'

    G: 'Make it nine chips.'

    A: 'Make it thirteen.'

    C: 'Make it twenty-one.'

The other three players all throw in, and C collects the pot. A is fairly sure that C is not bluffing, and is not prepared to risk another 8 chips. He played badly, of course, in raising G's nine chips to thirteen.

Tabular restatement

	A	B	C	D	E	F	G	Total
Chips contributed before the deal:	1	1	1	1	1	1	1	7
First Betting Round:				2	No	2	2	
	3	No	3	3		No	3	16
Second Betting Round:				(3)			4	
	4		4	4				20
Third Betting Round:							5	
	5		5	5				24
Last Betting Round:	5		5	5			9	
	13		21	No			No	
	No							52

C collects a pot worth 52 chips, of which 31 represent his profit.

SECOND EXAMPLE

This is a deal (based on an actual play) in which two exceptionally good hands came into conflict at the finish.

Each player having put up one chip, G dealt these cards:

	Exposed	*Hole Card*
A:	♣ 6	♢ 10
B:	♡ J	♡ 6
C:	♠ 7	♢ 3
D:	♣ A	♠ A
E:	♡ 4	♢ Q
F:	♠ 9	♣ 5
G:	♡ 8	♡ K

D (with an Ace exposed) was first to speak.

First Round Betting

D: 'Make it two chips.'
E: 'Two chips.'
F: 'No' (fold his cards).
G: 'Two chips.'

A: 'No' (fold his cards).

B: 'Three chips.'

C: 'No' (folds his cards).

D: 'Make it four.'

E: 'Four.'

G: 'Five' (the limit permitted).

B: 'Five.'

D: 'Five.'

E: 'Five.'

Both B and G are (fatuously) stepping up the betting because they have two cards to a flush.

Cards are now dealt to the four players left in the pot:

	Exposed	Hole Card
B:	♡ J 5	♡ 6
D:	♣ A 8	♠ A
E:	♡ 4 ♣ 4	◇ Q
G:	◇ K ♡ 8	♡ K

Second Betting Round

E, with a pair of 4's exposed, speaks first:

E: 'Check.'

G: 'Make it six chips.'

B: 'Make it seven.'

D: 'Make it eight.'

E: 'No' (abandons 5 chips).

G: 'Okay; eight.'

B: 'Make it nine' (the limit permitted).

D: 'Nine.'

G: 'Nine.'

Now there are two players, beside himself, to whom G must give cards. The hands are:

	Exposed	Hole Card
B:	♡ J 10 5	♡ 6
D:	♣ A 8 ◇ A	♠ A
G:	◇ K ♡ 8 ♠ 5	♡ K

D, with a pair of Aces showing, opens the betting:

Third Round Betting

> D: 'Make it ten chips.'
> G: 'Ten chips.'
> B: 'Make it eleven.'
> D: 'Twelve.'
> G: 'No' (folds up).
> B: 'Thirteen chips' (the limit).
> D: 'Thirteen.'

B and D receive their fifth cards from G. Their hands are:

	Exposed	*Hole Card*
B:	♡ J 10 5 2	♡ 6
D:	♣ A 8 ◇ A ♠ 8	♠ A

B has made his flush; D has made a full house.

Last Betting Round

D bets four chips (i.e., 17 in all). He does so because he thinks it must be obvious to B that he has made a full house, and that therefore there is no point in his checking in the hope of a raise. B, however, doubles (21 chips). D redoubles (29 chips) and B, at this stage has the sense to throw in.

D, very properly, does not show his hole card.

Tabular restatement

	A	B	C	D	E	F	G	Total
Chips put up before the deal:	1	1	1	1	1	1	1	7
First Betting Round:				2	2	No	2	
	No	3	No	4	4		5	
		5		5	5			23
Second Betting Round:					5		6	
		7		8	No		8	
		9		9			9	35

	B	D	G	Total
Third Betting Round:		10	10	
	11	12	No	
	13	13		44
Last Betting Round:		17		
	21	29		
	No			68

D collects a pot of 68 chips, of which 39 represent his profit.

Five-Card Stud: Oswald Jacoby's Advice

I propose to conclude this chapter with some excerpts from Oswald Jacoby's book. I believe that his advice on how to play this difficult game is as good advice as one could hope to get anywhere.

'When Stud is played properly real competition occurs in less than one hand in ten, and furthermore, when this real competition does occur, it is usually restricted to two players. As a result, ordinary Stud is more of a gambling game than a light pastime.

'However, for those who want to play it there are six basic rules which should be followed almost explicitly. If you do follow them, there is no guarantee that you will win, but if you do not follow them you are certain to lose. They are:

'*Rule I. Do not stay on the first round unless:*

(a) You have a pair;

(b) Your hole card outranks any card shown;

(c) Your hole card is as good as any card showing and your up-card is a nine-spot or better.
    Exception. Once in a while, if both your hole and up-card are higher than any card showing except that of the original bettor, you may stay.

'*Rule II. Do not stay if you are beaten in sight.*

In other words, suppose you stay with a nine-spot showing and a king in the hole. On the second round you draw a ten-spot and some other player draws an ace. Right at this point you should give up all interest in the pot, the reason being that:

(*a*) If you don't improve you can't beat the ace;

(*b*) If you do improve, the man with the ace may improve also and will beat you;

(*c*) And, most important, the man with the ace showing may have an ace in the hole. Whereupon, if you catch a pair, your bad stay is really going to prove expensive.

'*Rule III. On the fifth card, if you show the best hand, check — do not bet.* The reasons for this are:

(*a*) No player who can't beat what you show is going to call;

(*b*) If you have nothing extra in the hole and anyone calls you, he will have you beaten;

(*c*) If you do have an "Immortal" and check, someone may bet into you and give you a chance to raise him back; if you bet, the best you can hope for is a call'. (An 'Immortal' means a hand which is certain to win, irrespective of what cards other players may have in the hole.)

(*Note.* Mr. Jacoby goes on to say that this rule 'should be broken almost as often as it is kept'. His example however, introduces the complications of a Table Stakes game, and I will not quote it here.)

'*Rule IV. Do not bet into a possible "immortal" when the player with the possible "immortal" can raise you back.*
'*Rule V. The correct bet is the size of the pot.*'

This rule has obviously little relevance to the club game I have described above, but it should be borne in mind if you are playing in a private game where less restricted betting is permitted. 'When you bet less you make it too easy for people to stay, and when you bet more you immediately drive out all but the very good hands.' Finally: 'When playing with a limit you should bet the size of the pot until such time as the chips in the pot exceed the limit. From then on you should bet the limit.'

'*Rule VI. It is also considered unwise to reveal your hole card in this game.*'

Jacoby illustrates his sarcastic comment with a couple of amusing anecdotes; I will quote the second of them:

'The other story comes from Harpo Marx. Harpo was playing in a reasonably-sized game and had kings back to back' (i.e., one king exposed and another in the hole). 'A player on the other side of the table, showing the ace of spades, tapped' (i.e., bet all his chips) 'and Harpo, for some reason or other took a long time to make up his mind what to do. The other player became impatient, turned over his four exposed cards and held all five in his hand, saying: "Come on. Make up your mind." Harpo then said, "Don't rush me. And, what's more, put your cards back where I can see them". The other player obligingly complied, but this time the ace of clubs appeared instead of the ace of spades, so Harpo's problem was solved.'

Jacoby goes on to discuss the play of Stud Poker in a Table Stakes game, but the complex issues involved lie outside the scope of this chapter. But what he has to say about Limit Stud is apposite:

'The essential difference between Limit Stud and Table Stakes lies in the fact that in Table Stakes your principal aim is either to win the very big pots or not be in them;

whereas in Limit Studs there are no very big pots, and your aim is to build up the pot any time you think you may have the best hand, even though someone may actually have you beaten

'Furthermore, in Limit Stud, there is little percentage, if any, in wasting chips for advertising purposes. Thus if you are the high man in a Limit game, with something like a jack or a ten, and have a deuce or three in the hole, you might just as well turn your hand without betting. If you show an ace or a king, however, you should always open on the chance that everyone will drop.

'In a Limit game if you happen to hold a small pair back to back or an ace or king in the hole, and are one of the last players to act, you should raise. True, you may be betting into a higher pair, but nevertheless the chances favour your having the best two-card hand, and accordingly you should start to build up a large pot.

'The later betting is, of course, based on your observation of the relative strength and weakness shown by the different players and by the amount of money already in the pot. While it is not particularly good tactics to bet into a possible "immortal," the amount that such a procedure can cost you is nowhere near so great as it might be in a Table Stakes game. Hence, at any time you think you have the best hand, go ahead and bet.'

CHAPTER XI

SEVEN-CARD STUD POKER

THIS is the most difficult of the games described in this book. Generically similar to the 5-card Stud game, it offers more scope for the exercise of ingenuity, and it makes greater demands upon one's capacity to concentrate and to memorise the cards that have been exposed.

The Mechanics of the Game

The cards are dealt seven times (if necessary) and there are five betting rounds. Here is the procedure:

(1) A card is dealt, face downwards, to each player.

(2) A second card is dealt, face downwards, to each player.

(3) A card is dealt, face upwards, to each player.

Now the players inspect the cards which have been dealt to them face downwards, and there follows

(4) The first betting round.

The player who speaks first is — as in 5-card Stud — he whose card ranks highest (if it's the highest hand that will win) or lowest (if its a Misère Stud). If two or more players qualify, the first to bet is the player nearest to the dealer.

(5) When the betting is concluded, a card is dealt face upwards to each player, followed by

(6) The second betting round. As before, the player whose exposed cards are most promising speaks first.

(7) One more card is now dealt face upwards to each player who is still in the game, and

(8) The third betting round follows.

(9) The real fun now begins. Each of those still playing is entitled to discard one of the five cards he has in front of him, and will receive another in exchange. Before these cards are dealt, players must signify their requirements. Any player can, if he likes, elect to stand on his five cards; but, if he does so, he cannot subsequently alter his decision.

A player who wishes to exchange an exposed card receives, in exchange another exposed card. Similarly, a player who wishes to exchange one of the cards dealt to him face downwards will receive another card which is similarly dealt face downwards.

(10) The fourth betting round follows.

(11) The procedure is similar to that already described. Exposed cards can be exchanged for exposed cards; unexposed cards for unexposed cards. And now comes, as the climax of all these operations

(12) The fifth and final betting round.

An Illustrative Game

To make this sequence of operations crystal-clear, I will describe one illustrative game. I shall assume that there are seven players, and that each of them, before the deal, puts up one chip. I shall assume also that (as in our 5-card club game) checking is permissible; that no bet can be made of more than one chip until the last round; and that no more than four chips in all can be bet in any betting round save the last.

I will not complicate the issue by indicating what are the cards that any of the players hold. It may be either a high-hand game or a Misère Pot. The procedure is exactly the same.

(1) (2) (3) The first three cards have been dealt to the seven players.

(4) E speaks first. He checks; F, G and A check; B bets

one chip (making 2 in all). C and D throw in. E, F, G all put up another chip. A says 'Make it 3' and B counters with 'Make it four'. E, F and G play for four; A makes it 5 (the limit); B, E, F, G all put up another chip.

(5) Another card is dealt, face upwards, to each player.

(6) Now B has to speak first. B checks; E checks; F bets one chip. G puts up a chip; A says 'Make it 7'; B and E play for 7. F now says 'Make it 8' and G folds his cards, abandoning six chips. A plays for 8; B makes it 9 (the limit); E, F and A play for 9.

(7) A fifth card is dealt to each player, again face upwards.

(8) Third betting round. It is still B's privilege to speak first. He bets one chip (making 10 in all); E and F put up one chip; A makes it 11; B makes it 12; E and F play for 12. Now A makes it 13 (the limit) and the other three players all put up one chip more. At this stage there are 60 chips to play for.

(9) The first discarding round. A throws an exposed card; B elects to stand; E throws an unexposed card; so does F.

(10) Fourth betting round. E — who has to speak first — checks; F checks; A makes it 14; B makes it 15; E makes it 16. F by now has cold feet and throws in. A makes it 17 (the limit) and B and E play.

(11) Second discarding round. A exchanges a card, face downwards; B having already elected to stand, cannot exchange even if he wished to do so; E exchanges an exposed card; the card he receives marks him as out of the running.

(12) Last betting round. It is still up to E to speak first. He checks; A bets four chips; B bets another four chips; E throws in. A raises B by 8 chips; B makes it 8 chips more and A (who is by now offered odds of 14 to one) sees him. B wins and collects a pot worth, in all, 120 chips.

Let me summarise these proceedings in one of my by now familiar tabular statements:

	A	B	C	D	E	F	G	Total
Chips put up before the deal:	1	1	1	1	1	1	1	7
First betting round:					(1)	(1)	(1)	
	(1)	2	No	No	2	2	2	
	3	4			4	4	4	
	5	5			5	5	5	27
Second betting round:		(5)			(5)	6	6	
	7	7			7	8	No	
	8	9			9	9		
	9							44
Third betting round:		10			10	10		
	11	12			12	12		
	13	13			13	13		60
Fourth betting round:					(13)	(13)		
	14	15			16	No		
	17	17			17			72
Fifth (and last) betting round:					(17)			
	21	25			No			
	33	41						
	41							120

B collects 120 chips in all, of which 79 represent his profit on the pot.

This deal illustrates how expensive a club game played on these lines can be. C and D — both cautious players — had learned by experience that it generally pays to abandon a hopeless hand at the outset. But G, F and E were not eliminated till they had lost, respectively 6, 13 and 17 chips. and A, who not only had a good hand, but suspected B of bluffing, contributed more than half of the latter player's substantial winnings.

I will now offer a couple of illustrative hands (showing what cards were actually dealt) and will then give what advice I can as to how these difficult pots should be played.

FIRST EXAMPLE (HIGHEST HAND WINS)

Each player puts up one chip towards the 'pot' and cards are then dealt as follows (cards dealt face downwards in brackets):

$$\begin{array}{l}
\text{A: } (\spadesuit\,9\,3)\ \spadesuit\,5 \\
\text{B: } (\diamondsuit\,Q\ \heartsuit\,7)\ \clubsuit\,Q \\
\text{C: } (\clubsuit\,9\ \spadesuit\,2)\ \spadesuit\,J \\
\text{D: } (\heartsuit\,10\ \clubsuit\,10)\ \clubsuit\,5 \\
\text{E: } (\heartsuit\,K\ \clubsuit\,4)\ \diamondsuit\,6 \\
\text{F: } (\diamondsuit\,A\,8)\ \diamondsuit\,3 \\
\text{G: } (\spadesuit\,K\ \clubsuit\,5)\ \diamondsuit\,4
\end{array}$$

First betting round

B, who has a Queen showing, speaks first:

B: 'Make it two.'
C: 'No' (turns over his exposed card).
D: 'Two.'
E: 'Two.'
F: 'Make it three.'
G: 'No' (folds up).
A: 'Make it 4.'
B: 'Make it 5.'

Five chips is the limit, and D, E, F, A all play for five. Another card, face upwards, is now dealt to the five players still in the game. Their hands now are:

A: (♠ 9 3) ♠ 5 ♢ 5
B: (♢ Q ♡ 7) ♣ Q ♢ 9
D: (♡ 10 ♣ 10) ♠ 10 ♣ 5
E: (♡ K ♣ 4) ♢ 6 ♡ 4
F: (♢ A 8) ♢ 3 ♡ J

A will speak first; he has a pair of 5's showing. He is hoping, of course, for a flush. B has made a pair of Queens; D has done even better; he has three Tens. E, who would have done better to throw in in the first round, has a miserable pair of 4's. F, like A, is no nearer to his hoped-for flush. Moreover, there are already three Diamonds showing on the table.

Second betting round

    A: 'Make it 6.'
    B: 'Make it 7.'
    D: 'Make it 8.'
    E: 'No' (folds his cards).
    F: 'Eight.'
    A: 'Eight.'
    B: 'Make it 9' (the limit).
    D, F and A all play for 9.

The third exposed card is now dealt to the four players who are left in. Their hands are now:

A: (♠ 9 3) ♠ A 5 ♢ 5
B: (♢ Q ♡ 7) ♣ Q ♢ 9 ♡ 6
D: (♡ 10 ♣ 10) ♠ 10 ♣ 5 2
F: (♢ A 8) ♢ 3 ♡ J ♣ J

Third betting round

    F, with a pair of Knaves exposed, speaks first.
    F: 'Check.'
    A: 'Make it ten.'
    B: 'Make it eleven.' (A pointless raise.)
    D: 'Eleven.'

F: 'Eleven.'

A: 'Make it twelve.'

B: 'Make it thirteen.' (Fatuous. However, 13 is the limit.)

D, F and A all play for 13.

Now comes the *first discard*. A throws the $\diamondsuit$ 5 and receives the $\heartsuit$ A. B throws the $\heartsuit$ 6 and receives the $\clubsuit$8. D throws the $\clubsuit$ 5 (since two other 5's have already been exposed) and his vigilance is rewarded; he draws the $\heartsuit$ 2 and has now what is almost certainly an unbeatable hand. F throws the $\clubsuit$ J and receives the $\spadesuit$ 7.

Now the competing hands are:

> A: ($\spadesuit$ 9 3) $\spadesuit$ A 5 $\heartsuit$ A
> B: ($\diamondsuit$ Q $\heartsuit$ 7) $\clubsuit$ Q 8 $\diamondsuit$ 9
> D: ($\heartsuit$ 10 $\clubsuit$ 10) $\spadesuit$ 10 $\clubsuit$ 2 $\heartsuit$ 2
> F: ($\diamondsuit$ A 8) $\diamondsuit$ 3 $\heartsuit$ J $\spadesuit$ 7

Fourth betting round

A speaks first on his pair of Aces.

A: 'Check.'

B: 'Check.'

D: 'Make it fourteen.'

F: 'No' (folds up).

A and B play for 14.

The *second discard:* A throws the $\heartsuit$ Ace and receives the $\diamondsuit$ 10. B makes the only possible draw: to an inside straight. He throws his concealed $\diamondsuit$ Q, and receives (face downward) the $\clubsuit$ Ace. D says 'No card'.

Fifth betting round

There is no competitive betting. D, with a pair of 2's showing, speaks first. He bets four chips, on the off-chance that one or other of the players may see him, but both throw in; and D takes the pot without disclosing his hand.

Tabular Re-statement

	A	B	C	D	E	F	G	Total
Chips put up before the deal:	1	1	1	1	1	1	1	7
First betting round:		2	No	2	2	3	No	
	4	5		5	5	5		
	5							27
Second betting round:	6	7		8	No	8		
	8	9		9		9		
	9							43
Third betting round:						(9)		
	10	11		11		11		
	12	13		13		13		
	13							59
Fourth betting round:	(13)	(13)		14		No		
	14	14						62
Final betting round:				18				
	No	No						66

So what at one point looked like being an exciting contest fizzles out tamely. D has won a pot of 66 chips; his profit is 48.

In a private game, where bets amounting to half the pot, or even more are permissible, a good many more chips would have changed hands on these cards. B's pair of Queens, for example, might have cost him up to 100 chips. On the other hand, there would not have been so many players staying till towards the end. These club games, with restricted betting, can—as I have learned from experience —prove very costly if one begins with a promising hand that is eventually outclassed; one hasn't the opportunity to frighten away other players while one is on top of the situation. I think it wise to get out quickly if the odds are heavily against me, however rewarding an occasional win may be on a hand that started inauspiciously.

SECOND EXAMPLE (SEVEN-CARD STUD MISÈRE POT)

The conditions are those which obtain in my first example. As no player was ever in danger of making a flush, I shall make the play easier to follow by not indicating the suits of the cards dealt.

Each player, as usual, contributes one chip before the deal. The cards originally dealt are (concealed cards in brackets):

A: (8 4) 9
B: (K 10) 4
C: (5 2) 7
D: (K 6) A
E: (10 8) Q
F: (3 2) J
G: (J A) 3

First betting round.

D, with an Ace exposed, speaks first.

D: 'Make it 2.'
E: 'No' (folds up).
F: 'Two.'
G: 'Make it three.'
A: 'Three.'
B: 'No' (folds up).
C: 'Make it 4.'
D: 'Make it 5' (the limit).
F, G, A, C all play for five.

The second exposed card is dealt, and the players now hold:

A: (8 4) 10 9
C: (5 2) Q 7

D: (K 6) A 3
F: (3 2) J 6
G: (J A) 3 8

Second betting round

Again D speaks first.

D: 'Make it 6.'
F: 'Make it 7.'
G: 'Seven.'
A: 'No' (abandons 5 chips).
C: 'Seven.'
D: 'Make it eight.'
F: 'Make it nine' (the limit).

G, C and D all play for 9.

The third exposed card is dealt to the four players still in the game. Their hands are:

C: (5 2) 7 A Q
D: (K 6) A 3 4
F: (3 2) J 6 9
G: (J A) 3 8 K

At this stage D's prospects are obviously the brightest. The odds are better than 3 to 2 against his making a 6-high hand, and the odds are about 5 to 2 on his making an 8-high hand or better.

Third betting round

D speaks first.

D: 'Make it ten.'
F: 'Ten.'
G: 'No' (folds up).
C: 'Make it eleven.'
D: 'Make it twelve.'

F: 'Twelve.'

C: 'Make it thirteen' (the limit).

D and F play for 13.

Now comes the *first round of discards*. C throws his Queen, and receives a 3, which gives him a pat 7-high hand. D throws his concealed King and receives a Queen. F throws his Knave and receives an Ace. So the competing hands are now:

$$C: (5\ 2)\ 7\ 3\ A$$
$$D: (Q\ 6)\ 4\ 3\ A$$
$$F: (3\ 2)\ 9\ 6\ A$$

Fourth betting round:

D: 'Make it fourteen.'

F: 'Fourteen.'

C: 'Fifteen.'

D: 'Sixteen.'

F: 'Sixteen.'

C: 'Seventeen' (limit).

D and F play for 17.

Second round of discards

C stands pat. D throws his concealed Queen, and receives a King. F throws his 9 and is given a 5. He has achieved a 6-high hand.

The three hands are:

$$C: (5\ 2)\ 7\ 3\ A$$
$$D: (K\ 6)\ 4\ 3\ A$$
$$F: (3\ 2)\ 6\ 5\ A$$

Final betting round

D checks. If he bets four chips, one or other of the players is almost certain to call or raise him.

F bets 4 chips (21). C makes it 25. D throws in. F now makes it 33, and C calls him. F wins the pot, as, of course, he knew he was bound to do.

Tabular Re-statement

	A	B	C	D	E	F	G	Total
Chips put up originally:	1	1	1	1	1	1	1	7
First betting round:				2	No	2	3	
	3	No	4	5		5	5	
	5		5					27
Second betting round:			6		7	7		
	No	7	8		9	9		
			9	9				43
Third betting round:				10		10	No	
			11	12		12		
			13	13		13		55
Fourth betting round:				14		14		
			15	16		16		
			17	17		17		67
Final betting round:				(17)		21		
			25	No		33		
			33					99

C played very badly indeed in not seeing F at 21. If F is bluffing, he won't see any raise by C. The restricted betting limits make successful bluffing at this stage very nearly impossible. Hence C has virtually thrown 12 chips away.

Advice on Play

What advice can usefully be given as to how this difficult game should be played? I have studied carefully what the leading American authorities have to say, but the seven-card Stud games which they play are in several respects different from ours, and so only advice of a general character is relevant. And, again, they largely address themselves to betting techniques which are precluded by the cramping restrictions which the game normally played in our clubs imposes.

Maurice Ellinger, on the other hand, has some useful observations on play in which he postulates a game very much like the game I have described. He envisages a pot to which, before the deal, each player contributes ten chips, where the limit of raise before the last betting round is five chips, and where the limit of raise for the last betting round is ten chips. This is a game which is not, on the whole, dissimilar to that which I have described.

How does Ellinger recommend one to play in such a game as this?

Here is a summary of his 'rules for successful play': They are not, he says, 'very difficult'; but they 'require great powers of concentration to put them into practice successfully.'

(1) A player with a hand containing a pair in the first three cards should always bet the limit, and should continue to do so until the last bet of all, unless either (a) another player raises him, or (b) another player has a better hand on the table.

(2) Similarly, the limit should be bet where one's first four cards are four to a flush or four to a straight (unless the other cards exposed render one's success unlikely).

(3) If you have no pair among your first three cards, and someone else bets the limit, stay for one round. On the second round you should stay, unless some player has a pair showing on the table; and even then you should normally stay (a) if you have a pair; (b) if you have three cards to a flush; (c) if you have three cards to a straight; (d) if two of your cards are higher than the pair which you can see.

(4) On the third round you throw in, if the fifth card dealt to you hasn't improved your hand.

Prima facie reasonable though these rules are, I do not go all the way with Ellinger in thinking that they should always be followed. No doubt they have much to commend them in a game where everyone is playing carefully. But I have so often seen seven-card Studs (particularly Misère Studs, on which Ellinger's book has nothing to say)—I have so often seen them played by gamblers who, in competition with one another, raise the pot to its permissible limit from the word go. And, if one stays on what is probably the best hand, one may, in the final betting round, be sandwiched between two players who will go on raising one another until one can't afford to stay in. So my usual practice is to get out fast, losing only my initial chip, if the first three cards dealt me don't look promising, and to play this conservative game until (as should normally happen) I can stand up to the antics of the gamblers with equanimity.

What American experts have to say about seven-card Stud is unfortunately barely relevant to the game which we play here. They play a game which is in many respects different from ours; and their bets before the final round are not restricted as ours are. But Oswald Jacoby has produced some interesting, and—I don't doubt—authoritative calculations of the odds against improvement in various situations; and I reproduce these in Appendix E.

PART II

CHAPTER XII

BLUFFERY

THE word 'bluffery' is—so far as I know—'my own invention,' and, like many other words I have invented, has a precise significance. It doesn't mean bluffing; it means the whole complex of considerations which determine whether, in a particular situation, bluffing should be resorted to. This is a problem to which, more often than not, no definitive answer can be given; but there is a good deal that can be usefully said on the subject.

Bluffing at Poker is the factor which—added to the factors, always present, of chance and skill—helps to make the game so enjoyable. Every good game has this barely-definable something that makes it more than the mere exploitation of an approved technique. In Chess, the factor of chance is absent, and the same is true of a number of other games for two players: Draughts, Go-bang, the Russian card-game which I call Challenge; the difficult and complex game of Go which has long been a cult in Japan. But in all these games the best players bring something to bear which is more than a sound knowledge of their underlying technique: something that makes demands, not on their intellect, but on their imaginative capacity. No rules can be formulated which govern combinational or positional play in Chess, and the same applies, *mutatis mutandis*, to the other games that I have mentioned.

The same thing holds good in games which are primarily games of skill but embody also a considerable element of chance. Here I would cite Contract Bridge, where the best players are not only conversant with the principles of bidding and of card play, but, once again, are constantly reviewing their opportunities imaginatively. And there is an infinitude of other games which are to some extent comparable: Backgammon is one; others are card games. There is a high skill factor in such games as Solo Whist; Piquet; Option; Gin Rummy; Canasta; and in all of them technical perfection (were such a thing conceivable) needs to be fortified by the exercise of the imaginative faculties.

Bluffing has a comparable place in the Poker player's repertory.

Every Poker player who hopes to win consistently must bluff from time to time: there is no doubt at all about that. But Bluffs are of many different kinds, which will presently be discussed in detail. There are (a) what I call semi-bluffs (a simple example is the draw of one card where one starts with three of a kind), and (b) outright bluffs, which, if not called, will win a pot on a worthless hand.

In due course I shall attempt to formulate my own views; but, before doing so, I should like to cite the views of established authorities. The questions at issue are of such importance that we may as well begin by putting two or three experts into the witness-box.

My first witness shall be my old friend Maurice Ellinger, to whose book on Poker I contributed a preface a quarter of a century ago:

Here is what Maurice Ellinger says:

'The problem with which one is confronted after the buy can be put succintly as follows: Is my opponent's hand better than mine? If so, shall I attempt to bluff him? This is one side of the problem. You have also to decide whether your opponent is trying to put a bluff over on *you*. . . . If your opponent has doubled before the buy, it is always safe to assume that he has got a hand which justifies his doubling. Suppose, for instance, that you play on a pair of Queens and another player doubles and draws two cards. Under ordinary circumstances you must always assume that he has threes. After the buy, if you have not improved you must not see him unless you have some definite reason to believe that he is bluffing.

'The first question you should ask yourself is: Why should he attempt to bluff you? A player never bluffs before the buy, as this player may be doing, without some definite reason. . . . Some players will bluff before the buy when they are losing, but these are so few, and the conception is so unsound, that the possibility may be ignored. The sound reasons for which a player may have made a bluff raise before the buy are as follows:

(1) that he is having a run of luck, and therefore has his opponents frightened;

(2) that you (the person he is trying to bluff) are having a run of bad luck, and are losing a lot, and are therefore tending to be over-cautious;

(3) that you have not been seeing his bets, but have been trusting him to have spoken the truth.

'Of these three the third is by far the soundest, and, indeed, forms the theme of the First Golden Rule of bluffing, viz: *if an opponent fails to see a bet that you made when there was a possibility of his beating you, he should be bluffed at the very next opportunity.*

'Two examples will make this clear. (1) Your opponent opens a Jackpot; you come in afterwards, drawing one card to a bobtail flush. Your opponent buys three cards and chips; you fill your flush and double. Your opponent fails to see you. The very next time that that opponent is in a hand, and there is no other opponent behind him or between you playing, he must be doubled before the buy, whatever the hand. These automatic doubles, as they may be called, are not primarily designed to gain an immediate profit. In other words, do not be disappointed if your bluff fails. The real purpose of the scheme is to induce your opponent to view your bets with distrust and to see you in future whenever there is a possibility of his beating you. (2) You·open a Jackpot on three Aces. Your opponent, who could not open, draws one card. Two other players come in, drawing three cards each. You double, and none of the three players sees you. There are no indications that you should stage an automatic bluff against any of these three because you have no reason to believe that any of them had openers. . . .

'Now let us consider how one can detect when an opponent is bluffing. Here we have our Second Golden Rule. *If an opponent makes a bet which is not in accordance with his usual style of play, he should always be assumed to be bluffing.* By far the most common example of this arises as follows: A opens a Jackpot and draws three cards. B comes in, drawing three cards. C and D, neither of whom could open, come in, drawing one card each. A chips and B doubles. Now B is almost certain to be bluffing. He has two one-card buys after him made by players who must be going for flushes or straights. Therefore, unless he has made a full house or fours, he is taking an absurd risk by doubling. So it simply boils down to which is the greater probability: that he has made a full house or better, or that he is bluffing. The latter is so very much more probable that it can always be assumed. Now suppose that you are C or D, and have failed to fill your bobtail. Here you have an opportunity of perpetrating one of the most beautiful coups in the game of Poker, namely, redoubling. A is now in a very difficult position. Unless he is a good player, he will already be frightened by B's double. When he hears your redouble he is now convinced that he is beaten. This is one of the few cases in which even a bad player in A's position, who normally sees a hand as good as threes, will put them down and surrender the pot. B, of course, although he may have a better hand than you since he drew three cards, will be so obsessed with the idea that his bluff has failed that he will never dream of seeing you. . . .

'The Third Golden Rule is: *if in straight Poker all those*

*who are playing have drawn three cards and one of them bets,
always assume that he has improved his hand'.*

This third rule seems to me to be so little in need of
elaboration here that I don't think I need quote further.
For our two other witnesses let us, once again, cross the
Atlantic. Here is what Albert Morehead has to say:

'First, and most important, you have to bluff sometimes. I know that some players are temperamentally
unsuited to bluffing and find it repugnant, but is a necessary part of the game. If you never bluff, that fact soon
becomes noticed and you do not get called on your good
hands. If you never get called on your good hands, you
are unlikely to win.

'The literature of Poker takes a standard attitude
towards bluffing. "Bluffing is advertising" it shouts.
"When you bluff, expect to lose; your reward is that you
will then get called on your good hands."

'I have always agreed with the conclusion but I have
never been able to stomach the premise.

'In my opinion, every bet you make in poker should be
made for one purpose only: To win the pot. I admit that
bluffing is a losing game at best, because in Poker the best
hand usually wins the pot, but I still feel that every bluff
should be so designed as to have the best possible chance
to win.

'My advice on bluffing policy is as follows. At the start
of the game, do not bluff. If you are getting called on your
good hands, continue not to bluff. After two or three cases
in which you do not get called, begin to bluff. After two
cases in which you have bluffed and have been caught,
stop bluffing until again you find that you are not being
called on your good hands.'

I don't think one could go far wrong if one followed this
advice; but I can't help wondering if the tactics one should
employ in bluffing can ever be formulated with as much
precision as this. In the games in which I myself participate,

it's the good players one is pitting one's wits against; the duffers are easy money anyway. And the best players would very soon cotton on to the fact that one rationed oneself to a couple of bluffs at a time.

Albert Morehead's evidence is resumed:

'Scientific bluffing requires a knowledge of position. . . . Most of all, however, it requires a certain amount of conscious thought. It is not a matter of inspiration.

'Plan your bluff in advance. Imagine a particular hand that you would like to hold and imagine the most skilful way you could play that hand. Then, assuming that you hold the hand you wish to represent, bet throughout as if you held that hand. The most frequent bluff by far is also the most futile bluff. A player draws one card to a straight or flush possibility, fails to fill, and stubbornly bets away. This is a bad bluff for a liberal player. It is a good bluff only for a conservative player who almost never draws to a straight or flush possibility, and even that player must be careful not to bluff into a hand that may comprise two fairly high pairs, because his one-card draw will usually be figured for a two-pair hand. He will get a call that is not suspicious but quite valid.

'The next most frequent bluff, and almost as futile a bluff for a good player, is the one in which a player with a single pair represents three of a kind by raising before the draw and drawing two cards, after which he bets. If it is a planned bluff, he may have a two-card draw to a straight or flush rather than a pair. Before considering this bluff, make sure that if you actually did hold three of a kind you would play them in exactly the same way. A bluff must always be planned from the start of the hand. If it is based on a later impulse, it will hardly fool a good player because he will find some inconsistency in the way the hand was played at the start.'

Let me say, at this point, that I am in full agreement with Morehead's dictum that a bluff should be planned from the outset; it should seldom be improvised during the play of a hand. If you are in two minds whether to bluff or not, some hesitation or gesture — perhaps imperceptible to you — will be noticed by the most observant of your competitors. But if you can, like a well-trained actor, *think yourself into your part*, then you will play it naturally.

For example, I have been consistently successful with the bluff on which Ellinger, maybe, bestows excessive commendation: the bluff redouble following what looks like a bluff double. If my position at the table favours an attempt to bring off this *coup*, and if the people playing are 'tight' or unimaginative players, I say to myself — I'm thinking now of a Misère Pot — 'I'm going to be dealt a pat six, and if the pot is opened and doubled in front of me I shall promptly double again'. And, while I appear to look at my cards, I don't really take note of them; I think of them as constituting the pat six which I can see in my mind's eye. The bluff may be called, of course, by an original doubler who happens to hold a pat seven; but, if so, the money spent isn't wasted; the next time, and the time after that, I shan't attempt the *coup* till I really have a good hand. One can't forecast one's routine with precision; there are — let me repeat — so many imponderables.

Now let us proceed with Albert Morehead's evidence:

'This brings us to another cliché of Poker, but it is a valid one: It is easier to bluff a good player than a poor player. For example, a poor player will often stay in on a low pair and draw two cards to the low pair and an ace kicker. Don't try to bluff him by drawing two cards. He will be too suspicious of an unsound act that he is capable of doing himself.

'Always most effective among bluffs is the pat-hand bluff. It is most effective if you have simply played without raising when you are close to the opener or when there is obviously a chance that several players may stay or even raise after you. For this kind of bluff, if you do get a later opportunity you must raise, and, if the pot has previously been raised, you must re-raise. It is logical with a pat hand to try to suck in as many players as possible, and if there is any false note — if you would not have played a genuine hand in exactly the same way — it is a bad bluff.'

Morehead, I should add, is here discussing hands dealt in straight Poker, where, as we know (p. 80) the odds against being dealt a pat hand that is likely to win the pot are about five times as great as the odds against being dealt a comparable Misère hand. His views should be considered in the light of this all-important consideration

Finally, let the usher call Oswald Jacoby. Jacoby, I gather, regards Draw Poker as a poorish game compared with Stud Poker, but what he has to say of bluffing in the former game is very much to the point. It does not differ greatly from the opinions I have already quoted:

'In Limit Draw Poker — and practically all Draw Poker is played with a limit — a player should regard his bluffs in the same manner as a businessman regards his advertising appropriation. During the course of a session of play you have a certain number of winning hands. Naturally you bet with these hands, and naturally you want people to call you, since when they call they are giving you chips. However, if you never bluff, no one is going to call those bets, and hence you should spend a certain amount of money bluffing in order to get these calls.

'Of course once in a while a bluff will be successful and will win the pot for you. That is just gravy, since you should bear in mind that your bluffs are actually nothing but advertising.

'The most elementary and frequent bluff in Draw Poker is the bluff when you have drawn to a straight or flush and failed to make it. As a matter of fact, practically every player bluffs too often in this situation since the temptation is so great. Actually you should bluff about once for every ten or fifteen times you draw to this hand unsuccessfully. When you bluff more often in this situation you are putting too much money into your advertising budget. When you bluff less often you are going to lose a lot of calls when you have made your hand.

'The pat-hand bluff is one of the most effective I know and is really likely to succeed. There are three forms to this bluff. First the pot is opened right in front of you and you simply call. Now if anyone raises, you stand pat, and immediately all the other players think you surely have a pat hand and are sandbagging. After the draw you bet the limit and it really takes a stout heart to call you.'

(Compare these comments with Morehead's. Great minds are thinking alike. But there are interesting differences in their approach to the whole question of bluffing which, show how many facets the problems posed have.)

'The second variation: you raise before the draw and again stand pat. This second variation is by no means so advantageous as the first. Here is why: we will assume a total ante of seven chips and a five-chip limit. In the first instance the pot is opened for five chips. We call for five, leaving a total of seventeen in the pot. No-one else comes in. After the draw we bet five more. If we are called, the bluff costs us ten chips; if we are not called, we have gained twelve. In the second instance there is a chance that the opener will drop when we raise. However, assuming that he does stay, there are more chips in the pot. Hence he is more likely to call us after the draw. Furthermore, if this bluff is unsuccessful, we have lost fifteen chips.'

This argument maybe needs clarification. And how far does it apply to the pots which we have been discussing? I have thought it worth while to set out Jacoby's argument in more detail; and to add figures showing how the problem

presented in his pots compares with the corresponding
problem presented in our own:

Chips in the Pot	JACOBY'S POTS FIRST BLUFF Contributed by				OUR POTS FIRST BLUFF Contributed by			
	The Pot	Opener	Us	Total	The Pot	Opener	Us	Total
Before we call	7	5		12	14	4		18
After we have called	7	5	5	17	14	4	4	22
After we have raised	7	5	10	22	14	4	8	26
Loss if we are called				10				8
Gain if we are not called				12				18

Chips in the Pot	SECOND BLUFF Contributed by				SECOND BLUFF Contributed by			
	The Pot	Opener	Us	Total	The Pot	Opener	Us	Total
Before we raise	7	5		12	14	4		18
When our raise has been accepted	7	10	10	27	14	8	8	26
After our second raise	7	10	15	32	14	8	16	38
Loss if we are called				15				16
Gain if we are not called				17				22

Clearly Jacoby's argument applies *a fortiori* to our own
situation.

Our expert witness, Oswald Jacoby, will now conclude
his evidence:

'The third variation of the pat-hand bluff occurs when
you open, someone raises, and you now decide to raise
back, stand pat, and bet after the draw. In Jackpots this
particular technique is likely to prove effective since your
opponent will know that you have openers, at least, and
therefore will say to himself: "If he didn't really have a
pat hand, why wouldn't he try to draw against me?"

'A favourite bluff of many players is to raise on a four-
flush. They then draw one card and bet, whether they
make their flush or not. While this bluff must lose money
in itself, the player who makes it gets an awful lot of calls

when he starts with two big pairs or three of a kind and uses the same tactics.

'In addition to the above there are any number of complicated bluffing situations in many of which a player will actually get away with the pot, particularly if he makes his bluff against a good player of the cautious type. For instance, here is one example: Players A and B stay in a raised pot and each draws one card. After the draw Player A bets and Player B raises, whereupon there is a strong presumption that Player B has at least a high straight. Player A now raises back, purely as a bluff. Player B says to himself: "A must have at least a full house to raise me back", and throws away his hand.'

This last instance is not, I think, particularly relevant to games (like that I have described throughout) where there is a limited raise (8 chips). If successive bets could be increased proportionately to the mounting total in the pot, so that B had to put up (say) 32 chips to see A's final bet, the pot would only be offering odds of about four to one, and B would probably throw in. But in the game which I have described throughout, the pot is at this stage offering B odds of about nine to one: a very different proposition.

Readers have now heard our expert witnesses, and have (I hope) followed what they have to say with the concentration it deserves. *You have next to no chance of breaking even in your Poker games if you don't understand how much depends on an intelligent attitude towards bluffery.* I propose, therefore, to offer now my own conclusions. They are not based, primarily, on what the experts have to say but on my own observation and experience.

Here are, first, some preliminary generalizations.

(1) You are not well-equipped for Poker games if you are not prepared, on occasion, (a) to bluff, and (b) to be bluffed. The player who never bluffs will not be called if his bets suggest that he has the best hand at the table, save on the rare occasions where a hand that would normally win

happens to encounter a better one. And the player who refuses to be bluffed — who adopts the 'must keep you honest' attitude — may be performing a useful service to the table as a whole, but at heavy cost to himself. That can be stated categorically, and without any qualification.

(2) I agree with the proposition, already cited, that chips laid out in bluffing should be regarded as one's 'advertising appropriation'. One expects — taking one's bluff bets as a whole — to lose by them. As Jacoby says, if a bluff bet wins, it's just 'gravy'. But, if your advertising appropriation is intelligently laid out, it may well bring in a return out of all proportion to its actual cost. For one bluff that is exposed, half-a-dozen or more bets may be called which would otherwise pass unchallenged. Try, next time you play, to keep a mental record of what the bluffs you make have cost you, and what you have gained by creating the impression that your bets on winning hands are suspect. If there isn't a sizeable profit — taking the two transactions together — something has gone wrong. Try to find out what it is. Either (a) you are bluffing too much; or (b) some gesture or facial expression gives away the fact that you are bluffing; or (c) you are making bets which don't accord with your normal style of play, and one or more observant opponents has noticed this.

(But here let me remark, *en passant*, that if you are a top-ranking player you don't have a 'normal style of play' at all. Your tactics should be constantly changed, so that no one can truthfully say: 'In such-and-such a situation, X always does so-and-so.')

(3) The most important factor in the situation is one about which generalization is impossible. *How much do you know about the characteristics and the psychology of the other players at the table?* Is it a 'tight' game, in which players aren't taking risks on dubious hands? Or is it a 'liberal' game in which the majority of those participating are prepared to bet more freely? If the former, there is more scope for intelligently-planned bluffs.

Probably the six other players at your table constitute a mixed bag. If you are a club habitué, you should be well acquainted with their characteristic reactions to the various situations that arise. To take one example, you are playing against A, B, C, D, E, F. They are all well known to you, and you have formed the following opinions concerning each of them:

A is a forthright, honest-to-God, type who always bets the same hands in precisely the same way. For example, he never raises the opener of a Jackpot on a worse hand than two pairs; he doesn't stay for a re-raise if two pairs are all he has; he always buys three cards to one pair, but also (illogically) always buys one card to threes.

B is a reckless player who has more money to throw around than the other players at the table; he is almost always a heavy loser but regards his Poker losses as 'peanuts'. 'I just play for the fun of the thing' he tells you.

C is a shrewd player, on balance (you believe) a winner, but inclined to be careful of his money. You have never known him try to stage a counter-bluff against a player who is bluffing against him.

D is just a duffer who attributes all his misfortunes to 'bad luck'. He always plays (and stays) in Jackpots on a small pair; he will constantly draw two cards in Misère pots if he hasn't a one-card buy; if there are several other players in the pot, he is perfectly capable of drawing three. A welcome player at the table, many of whose members will listen to his hard-luck stories sympathetically.

E is a very 'tight' player. Having opened a Jackpot on 9 9 3 3, he will quit if another player doubles him; unlike A, he always buys two cards to threes, and never buys two cards except to threes.

F belongs to the 'must keep you honest' school. If he is in a pot, he is certain to see a bluff that another player puts up.

What should your tactics be against this representative assortment of players? If you have been dealt a good hand, you will sometimes raise the buy; you will sometimes re-raise another player; you will sometimes stand pat (e.g., on a Straight) and will give others the opportunity to raise and re-raise before you come into the open. But here I am considering bluffs. You will never try to bluff B or F, for B will cheerfully risk a few more 'peanuts', and F is a self-dedicated *vigilante*. You will think twice before trying to bluff D ('Bad players are less easily bluffed than good ones'). That leaves A, C and E, and an infrequent bluff against one or more of these players may well justify your outlay. These bluffs would not be mere 'advertising'; they would be bluffs *à la* Morehead, made in the expectation of winning the pot.

That's one side of the medal. The other is, of course: which, if any, of these players is likely to try to bluff you? Answer: B, C, and D. If, in the draw, you haven't improved your hand, surrender your chips without throwing any more away.

And, of course, you should add to your knowledge of each player's style of play, such special knowledge as you may have acquired by observing him closely — both when he is up against you and when he is up against other players. Pigeon-hole these data in your memory, and, from time to time, bring them up to date.

Finally, if the table includes one or more players whom you are opposing for the first time, don't try any 'funny business' till you have learned something about them.

Let us now consider, on their merits, the various bluffs and semi-bluffs which you may or may not have in your repertory; you may well encounter them — if you don't care for them yourself — in the repertories of others.

Semi-Bluffs

(1) IN THE ANTE AND STRADDLE GAME

If you have established a reputation for conforming, as a general rule, to the well-established principles for playing where there are only the conventional Ante and Straddle to play for, you may, now and again, think it worth while to depart from them. But such occasions are (or ought to be) few and far between, for, unless you are the Ante or Straddle, there is no point in playing in these pots at all. By any departure from the norm you are almost certainly risking more than you stand to gain. For example, to open on a bobtailed Flush, or on a low pair where you are one of the first four, has nothing whatever to commend it; any subsequent player with a good enough hand to double on will raise you before the buy, and then you must either sacrifice four chips or put up four more with the relevant odds heavily against you. And, as you will be first to speak after the buy, you will be laying yourself open to another double which may or may not be a bluff. I don't think more need be said about players who have no initial stake in the pot.

There is more scope for semi-bluff bids if you are Ante or (should the Ante be playing) the Straddle. The Ante will perhaps double before the buy, holding, say, a pair of Aces. If the Straddle accepts the double, the Ante should normally buy honestly, giving himself the best chance of finishing with the better hand. If 'sandbagging' is frowned on, he should then 'check dark'. If the Straddle has redoubled before the buy, this may or may not be a bluff; it's then up to the Ante to surrender eight chips; to accept the redouble; or—against a timid player—to double again and draw no cards. Frequent indulgence in these antics may prove expensive and they should not often be resorted to.

(2) ANTE AND STRADDLE, WITH
COMPULSORY OPENING

Here, as I remarked in Chapter IV, there is much more room for semi-bluff betting; with several 'sporting' players at the table it may become very expensive. For example, D—the first player to speak—has put up four chips before looking at his hand. The next player, E, promptly says, 'Make it eight'. F passes. G looks at his hand; he has, say, Knaves up: probably the best hand at the table. All the same, he is on the horns of a dilemma. If he plays for eight, there are still three players to speak, one of whom may raise the stake again. Suppose that D, having looked at his hand, says, 'Make it sixteen,' and that E immediately counters with, 'Make it twenty-four'. G would almost certainly be well advised to throw in. It may be that neither E nor D has, at the moment, as good a hand as his is (e.g., E has a pair of Aces and D has four cards to a Flush) but he—G—is in the unenviable position of being 'between the upper and nether millstones'. Where there is a good deal of loose play at the table—as there almost always is in this game—my experience favours staying out of pots in which I have no financial interest unless I have a really good hand.

No calculation of chances can normally be relevant.

(3) JACKPOTS

Here are two other types of semi-bluff bets:

(a) Bets made by the opener;
(b) Bets made by one of the other players.
(a) The opener has several semi-bluff situations to consider. These include:

(i) drawing two cards to a pair;
(ii) drawing one card to threes;
(iii) standing pat on a pair or on threes;
(iv) standing pat on two pairs;

—and in each case either doubling after the buy, or—if he has been raised before the buy—immediately reraising.

Let us consider each of these situations in turn.

(i) Drawing two cards to a Pair

So far as the opener of a pot is concerned, there is almost nothing to be said for this manœuvre. So many players attempt it so often that even a player who has only a pair of Aces, or a pair of Kings, is quite likely to call you; the pot will normally lay adequate odds. You may, of course, have improved your hand after the draw, and so be able to bet with confidence after the buy; though against many players you would do better to check after the buy and see what happens. If some other player has raised you, and you have accepted the raise, to draw two to a pair is usually suicidal. You are (as has already been pointed out) worsening the odds against you; they become three to one against your improving your hand, instead of only $2\frac{1}{2}$ to one; they become 12 to 1, instead of 8 to 1, against your making threes.

The only situation in which you should even consider staging this bluff is where a timid player—whom you place with two pairs—has raised you before the buy. If you re-raise before drawing; draw two cards; and raise again after the buy, a poor player may throw in. But these tactics are likely to fail against an intelligent player, because you are making a bet where, if you held threes, a bet would be wrong, against a one-card buy. In other words, you are making a bet which is out of character, and should therefore suggest a bluff.

These remarks have reference to a situation where you can, if you like, check. If you have to 'chip', i.e., put up a minimum stake, you are of course in a better position; if the chip represents as little as ten shillings it may be enough to prove a deterrent against a careful player.

(ii) Drawing one card to threes

This is a more intelligent type of semi-bluff. There are three points in its favour. (1) If you make this draw occasionally other players won't be able to tell whether you are drawing to threes or to two pairs, and won't raise you unless they have at least threes which are likely to be better than yours. (2) This play—effected occasionally—is a useful contribution towards one objective which you should always have in mind: keeping the other players guessing. Finally (3) it does not greatly lengthen the odds against success, except the odds against your getting fours. They are, in effect doubled; odds of $22\frac{1}{2}$ to one against you become 46 to one against you: a consideration worth bearing in mind if penalties are payable. But your odds against making a Full House are actually improved if you keep a kicker; they are shortened from $15\frac{1}{2}$ to one against you to $14\frac{2}{3}$ to one against you.

However, the net effect of this play is to increase the odds against improvement from $8\frac{2}{3}$ to one against you to $10\frac{3}{4}$ to one against you; so it should not be resorted to more often than seems desirable.

An important consideration, to my mind, is how high your threes are. If you have opened a Jackpot which four other players have entered, all of them drawing three cards, the odds are only three to two against none of them making threes; so if you have opened on, say, three 3's, you should give yourself the maximum chance of improvement. But if you have opened on three Aces, a one-card buy may result in a double from a player who has, say, three Queens.

Balancing all these considerations, I recommend that you should buy one card to threes occasionally: say, on balance, about once or twice in a session.

(iii) Standing pat on a pair or on threes

Standing pat on threes has next to nothing to recommend it, but standing pat on one pair is a manœuvre that one frequently sees succeed. A player doubles you before the buy: presumably on two pairs. You double back; he accepts your re-double; now, holding (say) a pair of Kings, you stand pat and make some sort of bet after the buy. To double again would normally be inadvisable; you are increasing a pot (at your own expense) where you are not holding the winning hand. But if you are allowed to chip, and you do chip in the normal way, a careful player will, as likely as not, throw his cards in. Of course, you have to show your openers, and a player who has seen you bring off this *coup* once is likely to remember it for a long time. So it should only be very sparingly resorted to.

(*iv*) *Standing pat on two pairs*

Since the odds against improving two pairs are $10\frac{3}{4}$ to one, you are losing little by attempting this semi-bluff occasionally. Everything depends on what you know about the players who are up against you. If your two pairs are small ones, and if there are (say) two other players in the pot, you can, from time to time, try this semi-bluff with fair prospects of success. You will, of course, follow it up by a double after the buy. If, now, the next player to speak has, say, Kings up, he will probably throw in, for there is still another player to speak who may put up another double. So now he's out of the way, and if the third player has only two pairs, or has failed to fill a flush or straight, he will throw in too.

Against this argument there must, of course, be set the important consideration that the odds against your having been dealt a pat hand are about 130 to one.

(*b*) *Bets made by players other than the opener*

So many situations fall for consideration here that to attempt to analyse them logically would be about as profitable as attempting to forecast what a number of monkeys in a cage would be likely to do next. There are seven players at the table, of whom the reactions of two or three may be more or less predictable; the others will be doing all they can to get the better of one another. Thus a double after the pot has been opened may mean: (1) that the doubler has a pair of Aces; or (2) that he has two pairs; or (3) that he has threes; or (4) that he has a pat hand; or (5) that he has a bobtailed flush. Not all of these are intelligent doubles but, it's unlikely that they are all intelligent players, and any of these doubles is possible: I have seen them all over and over again. A double on two Aces has something to commend it; if no other players enter the pot, the doubler can buy either two cards or three: he needn't decide till he has seen how many the opener buys. A doubler on two pairs is more or less *de rigueur* if the doubler is the first player to come in after the opener. A double on threes can't, normally, be wrong—unless they are very good threes and the doubler is 'lurking'. A double on a pat hand may drive prospective clients away, but it won't do so if the doubler is not known to be a tight player. And a double on a bobtailed flush, though definitely foolish—since it shortens the odds laid by the pot—is none the less frequently made and, if the flush eventuates, has been a useful piece of advertising.

So there's a whole range of possibilities to be taken into account, and, so far, we have only considered one player. It would take so many words—and would be so unprofitable—to consider analytically the possible ramifications of this situation that I won't pursue it farther.

(4) FREAKPOTS

In the type of club game with which I am familiar there is a fair amount of scope for semi-bluffs in Freakpots. The most frequent of such semi-bluffs are:

(*a*) Standing pat against one or more players who have all drawn cards where one holds only threes, or perhaps only a pair. If no one has made a Full House or better, this bluff may occasionally succeed, particularly if a player who has (say) high threes is not the last to speak and is afraid of being doubled again. And a Freakpot is very different from a Jackpot, in that the odds against being dealt a pat hand are only about 20 to one.

(*b*) Doubling a player on, say, three cards to a Straight Flush, and playing them confidently as though one holds three Aces. A player who holds only moderate threes isn't likely to see a second raise if he hasn't improved.

(*c*) Doubling on an open-ended straight or a bob-tailed flush and playing the hand as though one had doubled on Fours.

These, and similar semi-bluffs, should only be attempted infrequently and against players who are not playing too liberal a game. Indeed, the general considerations that have been put forward already apply throughout.

(5) MISÈRE POTS

In many club games, as has already been emphasized, the majority of those playing come in far too often where they have but two cards, and may even make a habit of buying three where there are a lot of chips in the pot. In these games it's hardly necessary to bluff at all; if you get— as you must get in the long run— your fair share of pat hands and of hands to which you can properly buy one card, you will show a good profit on your Misère Pot without trying any funny business at all. There is perhaps only one semi-bluff that seems to me worth while; that is the re-raise, when the original bet has been raised once already, on a hand that gives you alternative plays, if your re-raise is accepted, because the player who raised originally has to speak before you. For example, you hold (pat) 8 6 4 2 A. A opens; B plays; C doubles; D and E throw in. You are F. You now double again and everyone thows in except D who accepts your redouble. If D now draws a card, you will stand pat, with the odds about four to one on your winning. But if D doubles again, and subsequently stands pat, he has probably a hand which is not worse than 7-high. Well, that's just bad luck. But, if you throw your 8, the *a priori* odds against you are slightly better than five to one. For if D has 8 4 3 2 A, or 7 6 5 2 A, or 7 6 4 3 A, you will win if you draw a 7, and the *a priori* odds, should he hold any of these hands, are only about three to one against you.

But there is little scope for even these rough-and-ready calculations during the course of play. In Misère Pots, your knowledge of the other players, and close attention to what is going on, are far more important than mathematical knowledge.

CHAPTER XIII

MEET THE BOYS AND GIRLS

IF POKER were a game played by robots, automata, or electronic brains, it would be a very different game from that played in our card clubs. Every bet made before the buy would be made in conformity with a nice calculation of chances, modified only by the introduction of bluffery in situations which our robots, etc., fully understood. Every bet after the buy would similarly depend upon psychological assessments which our mechanical players would be fully capable of making. And all would have — what is seldom encountered in real life — the perfect 'poker face'.

But, in fact, we are concerned in our clubs not with automata but with living specimens of the genus *Homo sapiens*, and no two of them react to the same stimuli in precisely the same way. That's why Poker is so fascinating a game.

The Proper Study of Mankind is Man . . .

— and nowhere can he be studied by those who are interested in his psychological make-up more effectively than at the Poker table.

> 'What a piece of work is a man! How noble in reason! How infinite in faculty! in form, in moving, how express and admirable! in action how like an angel! in apprehension how like a god! the beauty of the world! the paragon of animals!'

— so writes that supreme enigma among men, Shakespeare. Yet in how many respects (the reflective Poker player must think) do his dicta need to be modified.

I propose, in this chapter, that we should pay a short visit to a (purely imaginary) card club, and study a few representative players. None of them is meant to depict any individual known to me, but that doesn't make them any the less worth consideration. I once published serially about a hundred 'Letters to Rosalind', and I received a number of letters asking: 'Is Rosalind a real person?' My reply was usually that people could be 'real' in more senses than one. 'Rosalind and her family are much more real people to me than are most of the individuals I have lunch with.'

So let us visit what I will call Feste's Club. This is a cock-and-hen club; we shall meet the boys and girls. I use the term advisidly, for most Poker addicts seem to me to be young at heart. You can't play this difficult game if your faculties are beginning to atrophy.

A post-prandial session is in progress, and three full tables have been formed. At the first, Tybalt is about to deal the cards. TYBALT is, on the whole, a successful player. He is not in the top flight, for he has little imagination, but he knows his mathematical odds; he bluffs very little; when he does bluff he chooses his victims intelligently and quite often his bluffs aren't called. But he loses money — as do almost all his fellow-members — by making too many two-card buys in Misère Pots.

To his left sits the dignified VOLUMNIA. She has been playing Poker for fifty years, and has, unfortunately, done little to adapt her game to changing circumstances. The standard of play nowadays — though no one could call it high — is a good deal higher than it was when Volumnia was a girl. Almost all her actions in given situations are predictable; for example, if she has opened a pot on two pairs, she invariably bets six chips. You can safely raise her if you hold threes; you'd be a fool to see her if you have only two pairs. She tries about one bluff every session, and any observant adversary can tell when she is bluffing. I estimate that her Poker costs her about £20 a week.

OLIVIA, on Volumnia's left, isn't quite such easy money.

Olivia's in business, and is well-off; she has learned not to throw money away too readily. Her main fault, I think, is a tendency to 'linger' in pots that she has next to no chance of winning.

Next to her is IAGO: not a popular player, for, when in vein, he tends to drive his luck too hard, and too often makes sarcastic comments when others play ineptly. A master of low cunning, he yet lacks balanced judgment, and can often be trapped by what looks like a bluff but isn't.

GERTRUDE, his neighbour, detests Iago, and is hoping that there will soon be a vacancy at another table. She lacks equanimity. A few successful *coups* will unbalance her judgment; her winnings will begin to melt away; then she will become demoralized. After every failure she demands sympathy for her 'bad luck'; the response is discouraging, but it doesn't discourage Gertrude. There will be a general sigh of relief when she does contrive to change her table.

A very different type is Gertrude's other neighbour, CORIOLANUS. You will find his name in Burke's peerage, which will also tell you that his family's motto is *Semper audax*. Not a bad motto for a Poker player. But Coriolanus, playing for higher stakes than he can properly afford — he has already gambled away a couple of Gainsboroughs — plays exactly the type of game that ensures continuing failure: he gets cold feet where he ought to take risks, and takes unjustified risks where he ought to keep out. So his losses, though never spectacular, can add up to a formidable total. And neither his stand-offish manner, nor his lack of any sense of humour, adds to his popularity.

PERDITA, on Tybalt's right, completes the table. Perdita is a kittenish type whose well-to-do and indulgent husband pays her card-debts without a murmur; where Perdita loses £50, her quick-witted Florizel knocks up £500 on the Stock Exchange. 'I suppose I'm a silly girl, really,' giggles Perdita, drawing two cards in a Misère Pot. 'How many bones have I had so far, Gobbo?'

'Four, madam,' says Gobbo.

'I thought as much. I'd better have another one. And ask Audrey to take a round of drinks.'

I predict that there'll be three winners at this table: Tybalt; Olivia and Iago. Volumnia and Perdita will be the heaviest losers.

At an adjacent table CASCA is about to deal. Casca wants to win too much too quickly; when he bets or raises he seldom gets a re-raise. There's another mixed bag of players at this table: the aged LEAR, whose reactions have become so slow that he makes frequent (and expensive) mistakes; the petulant TITANIA, who can't be (and therefore never is) bluffed; the aggressive MACBETH, who begins by over-betting his hands and then loses his nerve. His wife (playing at Table 3) is keeping an eye on him; her expression now and again is one of near-contempt. She is well aware that he is not the stuff heroes are made of:

> 'Letting "I dare not" wait upon "I would,"
> Like the poor cat i' the adage.'

OTHELLO is Macbeth's neighbour; he too is an aggressive player, but totally lacking in guile; many a *coup* has been devised to relieve him of his money. Incapable of realism, he sees himself, not as the gullible victim of crafty little swindles, but as a man of untarnished integrity fighting against desperate odds.

JESSICA and GONERIL complete the table. Everyone likes Jessica; her charming little face is a joy to look upon; the more so, as it's an infallible guide to the value of her cards. She tries in vain to stage a successful bluff; some spoil-sport always calls it. And no one likes GONERIL, who plays too tight a game; counts the chips she has collected whenever she wins a pot, and often complains that someone is a chip or half a chip 'shy'. I suspect that Casca will be the big winner at this table, and that Goneril will be the runner-up.

At Table 3 there ought to be two winners; LADY MACBETH, who has courage, imagination and an eye to the main chance, and IACHIMO, who can out-smart most of his competitors, but impairs his prospects of winning much by never making a generous gesture. Possible winners are PORTIA, who plays a sound but unimaginative game, and BEATRICE. Beatrice is intelligent and vivacious; a star danced when she was born. She would be one of the club's most successful players if she could suffer fools gladly or resist the ravages of boredom when she's having a run of bad cards.

The other three players all lose in the long run. ROMEO is vain and impulsive. He overplays his good hands and makes no effort to limit his loss on poor ones. AUTOLYCUS is crafty but not intelligent; he risks too much to win a small pot, and often burns his fingers. The game is too high to give his tactics much scope. And HAMLET, though perhaps the most intelligent player at the table, is that psychopathic type: the dedicated gambler. Hamlet, though he doesn't know it, is in fact *playing to lose*. Gamblers of his type can never be winners; but, when they have lost all they can afford, they undergo a species of catharsis; they attain temporarily a sense of well-being comparable to that induced by the tragedies of Sophocles and Aeschylus.

The above is, I think, a not unfair picture of a totally imaginary but representative card club. It should help to explain why Poker players who lack many of the qualifications which the toughest games demand can — for short periods at any rate — contrive to hold their own. The problem that confronts the really well-equipped player is that of winning enough to make his efforts worth while, while not winning so much that before long the game will peter out altogether.

CHAPTER XIV

TRANSATLANTIC WISDOM

BEFORE I offer, in my last chapter, my own advice on how Poker should be played, I should like to assemble the views of three famous American experts. All these gentlemen — Oswald Jacoby, Albert Morehead and John R. Crawford — have been kind enough to give me permission to quote freely from their books.

1. The Wisdom of Oswald Jacoby

'A poker pot might well be compared to a building. First we have the ground on which the building is located, or the ante; then we have the foundation, or first-round bets; then the middle structure, or early-round bets; and finally the superstructure, or last-round bets.'

(The reference here, of course, is to Stud Poker; but the advice which follows applies equally to Draw Poker.)

'A beginner at Poker should have a sound foundation at all times. The very best Poker players do not always have this sound foundation, but if you sit in back of a good player for an evening, you will be surprised to see on how few bad hands he wastes even one chip; and when he does waste this one chip it is strictly for advertising purposes.

'Then we come to the middle-game or main structure. If his hand is not developing as well as his opponents' seem to be, watch the good player abandon the few chips he has already put in the pot and get out quickly. The fact that his foundation may have been supersound means nothing to him if the middle-game developments are unfavourable to him and favourable to the other players. *Remember, once a player puts chips into the pot, they cease to be his and merely represent an investment. If the investment starts to turn out badly, it is only a losing player who wastes more chips in an effort to protect it.*

'Finally we come to the superstructure, and here is where the expert really shines. Other players may build their foundation and middle structure just as well as the expert, but on those hands where a large final bet is called it will be found that the expert wins much more than half the time, while if a successful bluff is worked, the expert is much more likely to be on the right side of it than the ordinary player. The reason for this is that the expert is a psychologist. He is continually studying the other players to see, first, if they have any telltale habits, and, second, if there are any situations in which they act automatically.

'In connection with general habits I divide Poker players into three classes, namely: the ingenuous player, the tricky or coffee-housing player and the unreadable player.

THE INGENUOUS PLAYER

'When the ingenuous player looks worried he probably is worried. When he takes a long time to bet he probably doesn't think much of his hand. When he bets quickly he fancies his hand. When he bluffs he looks a little guilty, and when he really has a good hand you can see him mentally wishing to be called. This ingenuousness, incidentally, is seldom found in veterans. A player of this type usually quits Poker at an early stage on account of his "bad luck".'

THE TRICKY OR COFFEE-HOUSING PLAYER

'At least ninety per cent. of all Poker players fall into this category. The tricky player has a great tendency to act just the opposite of the way he really feels. Thus with a very good hand he trembles a little as he bets, while with a poor hand he fairly exudes confidence. Of course he may be triple-crossing, but year in and year out I have played in a great many games and have found that at least two times out of three when another player makes a special effort to look confident he has nothing, while when he tries to look nervous he is loaded.

'There is one little coffee-housing habit that practically never fails to act as a give-away. That is, showing too much nonchalance. For instance, it is my turn to bet and as I am about to put my chips in the pot one of the other players casually lights a cigarette. Experience tells me that this casual player is at least going to call me and is very likely to raise me if I bet. Accordingly, if I do see that sign, unless my hand is really very good I refuse to bet for him and simply check.

THE UNREADABLE PLAYER

'This particular individual is, of course, the hardest opponent of all. Invariably he knows the rules of correct play but departs from all of them on occasion. Unlike the ingenuous player, who acts the way he feels, or the coffee-houser, who acts the way he doesn't feel, this player has no consistency. Accordingly the fact that he exudes confidence or looks nervous gives no clue to the nature of his hand.

'When there is such a player in the game I endeavour as much as possible to steer clear of him. But if I do find myself in a pot against him I have found one method which works reasonably well. That method is to relax completely and then see if some impression is conveyed to me in a subtle manner. Then, having secured this impression, I act directly against it. In other words, if the impression is that he is bluffing, I may drop; if the impression is that he has a good hand, I may call. . . .

LUCK

'In any one session of Poker the Goddess of Chance is the one who determines the winners and the losers. In two or three sessions she has a lot to say about who wins. But over a long period she bestows her favours equally, and the good players win and the poor players lose.

'A Poker player might well divide his game into two parts: (1) the psychology, already discussed in this chapter; (2) the technical. I have already mentioned the fact that the really good Poker player must depart from correct technical play sufficiently often so that his opponents can never be certain as to what he is doing. Nevertheless, the technical side is far more important than the other; and while correct technical play will not make you a winner, it will certainly keep you from being much of a loser even against the best Poker players in the world.'

2. The Wisdom of Albert Morehead

Here are some extracts from Mr. Morehead's *Advice to all Players*.

ETHICS AND ETIQUETTE

'Poker is not a sociable game but it is distinctly a *social* game. That is, it is a game one must play with others, and we may assume that every human being would rather be popular than unpopular and also that every group will soon reject a player who is generally disliked by the other players. Therefore, if you are playing in a Poker game and you want to keep on playing, it behoves you to conform to the social customs of the game and make sure that the other players do not hate you enough to kick you out.

'It is notably unprofitable to be recognised as a good fellow in Poker games, but it is almost as bad to be characterised as a prime sonofabitch. The object of the winning player is to steer a middle course. He wants to be known as a tough but fair opponent, as a ruthless but honest adversary. The problem is, "How to be honest and yet a winner." My advice is as follows:

'(1) Sandbagging is a logical part of the game to the thinking player, but for some reason it enrages the average player. . . . Find out what the custom of the game is and observe it. If it makes the opponents mad for you to check the best hand and then raise, don't do it. It may slightly restrict your style, but it doesn't really have a great effect on your winnings or losses in the long run. In fact, much money is lost by failure to bet the best hand, in the vain hope that someone will bet into you.

'(2) In some games any comments you make are taken with a grain of salt, in other games the gentlemanly code is adopted and you are not supposed to say that you have a bad hand when you have a good one, that you filled a flush when in fact you didn't, etc. In such games, don't compromise your popularity by violating the customs. You won't lose anything by keeping your mouth shut; the bet speaks for itself anyway.

'A woman wrote to Dorothy Dix and said: "Dear Miss Dix: A man wants to marry me but he doesn't know that I have false teeth. Should I tell him?" Dorothy Dix answered with classic succinctness: "Keep your mouth shut."

'Since the Poker player would be a fool to tell the truth about his hand and may win undying popularity by playing the gay deceiver and the chatterbox, this is good advice for the Poker player too.

'(3) Be just a little more conservative than the standard established in the game. In all except the toughest games, the majority of players are more liberal than they should be. From curiosity, boredom, or sheer ignorance, they play too often, raise too often, and call too often. It is neither winning style nor good etiquette to become known as the Rock of Gibraltar in such games. . . . *It is true that conservatism pays in Poker, but don't try to make it pay too much.*

'(4) Conform to the pace of the game. . . . If you are by nature a slow thinker you may suffer a bit in the fast games, but not as much as you will suffer from violating the custom of the game.

'(5) Don't be a stickler for the laws in an amateur game.

The players commit the most horrible crimes known to Poker. They drop out of turn. They want to look at your hand when you bet and didn't get called. They relinquish a pot and then want to claim it when they find that they had the best hand after all.

'Let them get away with it. I assume your principal desire is to be a winning player . . . and in such a game you will be a winning player just by avoiding the more horrible of the mistakes that are made all around you. Be content with that. . . ."

This advice applies, obviously, to friendly games where you are one of the guests. In club games, the more heinous offences will be penalised; e.g., to 'drop' (throw your hand in) out of turn is a very serious offence and should, at least, meet with a reprimand.

'(6) Lose a few arguments. For example, if you have put in your ante and someone says you haven't, why not put it in again? On this subject I would like to make one sage observation. If you argue and then give in reluctantly, you have done just as much damage to yourself as if you argued and never gave in. In fact, you have done more damage; if you decide to stand on the fact that you are right, you may win the admiration of some players. Equally you will win their admiration when you give in fast and graciously although it is obvious that you were right all the time. . . . So you must either stand on your rights or yield with no murmuring or muttering, and you shouldn't do either of them all the time.

'(7). The traditional problem of etiquette is saved for last: Can you quit when you are a big winner?

'Here again the answer depends on the game. In a public game you should have no qualms at all; in a club game you should take care to give ample advance notice, such as a half-hour or an hour; and in a truly social game you mustn't. You can nurse your stack and you can refrain from doing anything that would keep the game going, but you can't give the impression that you are in there for the money and not for the sheer fun of it. At least wait till someone else quits and then go along with him.'

JUST HOW IMPORTANT IS MATHEMATICS

(I have already quoted, in Chapter II, what Morehead has to say on this fascinating question.)

PSYCHOLOGY AND BLUFFING

(Here again—in Chapter XII—I have summarised Morehead's advice.)

POSITION

'Position in Poker is a matter of the number of players who can still act after you. Playing position is a matter of taking into consideration what those players may do, before you decide what to do yourself.

'Position is a mystery to most Poker players. But next to the relative value of your hand it is the most important thing for a Poker player to think about in the game.

'In a Poker game you will have bad hands, fair hands, and good hands. The bad hands you will throw away. The very good hands will win for you, but you will not hold them often. . . . The fair hands represent the bulk of your winnings and losses, and your success in playing the fair hands will depend very largely on your understanding of position.

'Cases constantly arise when you consider your position as well as your hand, but at all times there are two main positional objects: First, you want to be last to act if possible. Second, you don't want to get caught between two players who have betting or raising hands. In a close case, you play along when your position is good and you drop when your position is bad.

'Take a case in draw Poker in which there will be at most three active players, whom we will call A, B and C. A has opened and B has raised. C should either re-raise or drop. If C simply calls, his position is bad. The normal process will be for A to check after the draw, and for B to bet. Now if C calls, even though he may think he has B beaten, he risks the danger that A can beat him and may even raise back. However, if C re-raises before the draw he makes his position good because A and B will normally check to him after the draw and he can have a free checkout if he has not improved. . . .

'A good bluff depends more on position than on any other factor. Strangely enough, it is not the usual "good" position that you want for a successful bluff; more often you want what would ordinarily be a bad position. For example, when there are four players in the pot the last player is in a fair position for playing a fair hand but in a bad position for bluffing. Those other three players, who checked him, all have a right to call and because they all checked none of them is afraid of any of the others. . . .

MONEY MANAGEMENT

'Seasoned Poker players will usually assure you that money management is at least as important as any other factor in skilful play. Many of them say it is the most important single factor. I am going to start this section with a few general but absolutely essential statements.

'First, the factor of *courage*. Here I will quote from a book by the celebrated card expert, John Crawford, because I could not possibly say this better:

> "A winning player must have a combination of two qualities. They are knowledge and courage.
>
> "The knowledge part is what you can read about in books.
>
> "The factor of courage can't be taught, but you can't win without it. When you get into a poker game, you arent' there to keep from losing. You're there to win. *And to do that you must back your good hands to the limit, and risk your money when you think you're right.*
>
> "This lack of courage is the reason so many Poker

players are at a disadvantage once they start losing. Every time another play bets aggressively, their first reaction is one of fear. They check when they should bet, and drop when they should call, thus winning too little on their good hands and losing on too many of their fair hands.

"I have known men who were formerly good Poker players but who lost their courage. . . . They promptly changed from good players to poor ones. If the amount of money at stake is frightening you, I can only recommend that you appropriate a certain amount of money that you are able to lose and play that money as though it were an unlimited supply. If you lose it all, quit the game. While you're playing you'll have a chance to win."

'That ends the quotation from Crawford and brings up the factor of capital. Proprietors of gambling houses used to say that "a sucker will sit and lose more than he will sit and win." It is necessary to limit your losses. *When you are losing you are probably an inferior player anyway;* your standards are distorted in your anxiety to get even. *The most widespread of mistakes in money management is to quit a game when ahead and sit out long hours of a futile losers' game when behind.* . . .

'Always use the same method of money management. A method of play is either right or wrong. If the method isn't right, you shouldn't adopt it in the first place. If it isn't right, you shouldn't deviate simply because you are feeling down in the dumps on account of your unlucky streak or over-conservative because you want to hang on to your winnings. A good rule is this. The first time you find yourself doing something midway of the game that you wouldn't have done on the very first hand . . . that is a good time to quit the game. (*In appraising your game, be honest with yourself.*)

'I would like to add just one personal comment on money management. Nothing upsets it so much as playing a "friendly game" in which there are certain players against whom you are not supposed to do your worst. To make the percentages work correctly, you have to be able to win the maximum when you have a winning hand, no matter whether the player with the losing hand is your friend or your enemy. It is unethical—worse, it is considered a form of cheating as bad as stacking the cards—to enter into collusion with another player to trap a third, therefore you have no compensating gain from your friendly agreement. It isn't always possible to avoid such situations, but stay away from them as nearly as you can.'

(3) **The Wisdom of John Crawford**

I have just reproduced a quotation by Morehead from Crawford's fascinating book, *How to be a Consistent Winner in the most popular Card Games*. Crawford's advice is, in general, on very much the same lines as Morehead's, so I will content myself here with quoting his

TEN THINGS EVERY WINNING POKER PLAYER MUST KNOW

This is the Crawfordian decalogue:

'1. You figure to lose unless you have the best hand going in.

'2. Treat every bet as though it were your first one— forget the money you put in the pot before.

'3. Call only when your hand should be good enough to win, not merely because you suspect a bluff.

'4. Don't try to bluff a poor player, a heavy winner, or a heavy loser.

'5. Drop a doubtful hand if you may later be in the middle between two strong hands.

'6. Most Stud players would win instead of lose if they never tried to draw out against an open pair.

'7. Raise on an early round to avoid calling a big bet later.

'8. A loser will drop a close hand if raised early, a winner will stay in.

'9. When you're sure you'll win a Stud pot, wait till the last round to raise.

'10. The more wild cards and crazy rules, the greater the expert's advantage.'

> — *If, reader, you would pass the tyro's test,*
> *Read, mark and learn, and inwardly digest.*

CHAPTER XV

CONCLUSION

This book has been written, in the first instance, for the thousands of Poker addicts who play the game regularly in reputable card clubs. I assume that the great majority of such players are playing to win, despite the participation in many games of players — described in Chapter XII — who are so well off that they can afford to play 'for fun', or of psychopathic gamblers who — perhaps unconsciously — are playing to lose. So I'll begin this concluding chapter by listing the qualities which the player needs to have who aims at being a consistent winner against tough opposition. And a formidable list it is.

1. COURAGE. Like John Crawford, I put this quality first. And what does *courage*, in a Poker game mean? It means *the refusal to abandon what one believes to be sound principles of play because the luck happens to be running against one.* If your financial resources are so limited that a run of bad luck compels you to play a restricted or a timid game, you shouldn't be in that particular game at all. Quit before you have lost everything.

2. CONCENTRATION. I know of no card game which demands concentration to the same extent as Poker. Even when you are not playing in a pot, you should be taking note of what other players are doing; otherwise you may miss some inference which you can presently turn to advantage. On the other hand, everyone's capacity for concentration is limited; in the course of a long session it may be more profitable to relax occasionally (when one is not oneself

playing) than to tire oneself by observing minutely what happens in every deal.

But loss of concentration during even one deal in which you yourself are participating may make all the difference between getting up a winner and getting up a loser.

3. OBSERVATION. *Concentration* and *observation* go hand in hand. The former quality allows you to exploit the latter to the full. How often one hears it said: 'I didn't notice how many cards you drew'. Such lapses may, in the course of a session cost a poor player hundreds of chips.

4. MATHEMATICAL KNOWLEDGE. I have said a good deal already about the extent to which mathematics are important. No-one who is not interested *as a mathematician* need bother about many of the speculations which you will find in Appendix E; but you *must* know what the rough-and-ready odds against you are in a number of familiar situations, and you *must* be capable of calculating whether, in any given situation, the pot is offering you longer odds, for only in such cases are you justified in playing. And you should (following Jacoby's advice) get out while the going is good from any pot in which odds which began by being promising have, as the betting proceeds, become adverse.

5. PATIENCE. (This is the quality which I have always lacked myself, and, I daresay, always shall lack). *Poker can be a damned dull game*, and, if you are not prepared to endure its dullness, don't expect to be a consistent winner. In Ante and Straddle games, where five players out of seven need risk nothing at all, you must be prepared to throw in hand after hand; the same is true of Jackpots and also of Misère Pots, for in Misère Pots you should hardly ever buy more than one card.

> 'Still achieving, still pursuing,
> Learn to labour *and to wait.*'

'Learn to wait'. Here is a pearl of great price to Poker players embedded in Longfellow's farrago of platitudes.

6. PSYCHOLOGICAL INSIGHT. Betting before the

buy should be primarily based on mathematics; betting after buy, on psychology. You are playing in a pot against Mr. Frog, Mrs. Mouse and Anthony Rowley. How much have you learned about their respective betting techniques? Are you aware that Mr. Frog invariably draws one card to threes; that Mrs. Mouse, similarly, always draws two cards to a pair; that Anthony Rowley, holding two pairs, doubles before the buy; stands pat; and then doubles again? Here's the material for a whole range of inferences which — if you're a good player — should go far towards winning the pot. And have you contrived, of set purpose, to give them comparable (but fallacious) impressions about your own style of play of which you feel fairly sure they will try to avail themselves? If so, you are in a strong psychological position, and the pot should be yours — even if you don't hold the best hand — maybe three times out of five.

All intelligent 'bluffery' has a psychological foundation, and I've done my best, in Chapter XII, to explore various bluffs and semi-bluffs in the light of this assumption.

7. IMAGINATION. A player lacking imagination may, if he has other qualities *in excelsis*, be a consistent winner, but he's not likely to win very much. Imagination, in this context, is the capacity to turn to account a particular situation by improvising an appropriate *coup*. In the game of skill which transcends all others — Chess — the opportunity to play imaginatively occurs in the so-called middle game, where *a priori* analysis is no longer relevant; Capablanca, Alekhine, Niemzovitch were imaginative players, as are Reti, Gligoric and Tal to-day. Poker offers comparable if less exalted opportunities; a situation will unexpectedly present itself in which, if you have imagination, you can evolve a line of play that is almost certain to succeed. *But only if you have judged the situation correctly.* Your *plan may* fail against players who, like you, have imagination and so can envisage what you have in mind; and it's almost certain to fail against stupid players who aren't using their brains at all. Against duffers, the subtler devices in your repertory

are almost useless. But that doesn't matter at all; because duffers will be losing enough chips anyway to compensate for their imperviousness to finesse.

8. CARD MEMORY. This is of small importance in Draw Poker where you don't, until the showdown, see anyone else's cards; but it is supremely important in all varieties of Stud Poker. Suppose you are playing Five-Card Stud; the 'moment of truth', when you're about to make your last bet, has arrived. Your four exposed cards are K K 6 6; you have another 6 in the hole. The only other player who has a chance of beating you is showing the Q J 10 8 of Spades. He has been betting confidently, and the 64-dollar question now poses itself: has he the ♠ 9 in the hole? Unfortunately, you have failed to memorize the fact that the ♠ 9 was in one of the hands already folded. And — as Morehead observes — 'you can't memorize a card you haven't seen'. You check; your opponent makes a limit bet; another player, who *does* know that the ♠ 9 is out, raises him on a straight, and, discouraged, you throw in.

You don't need, in a Stud game, to memorize *all* the cards that are folded; but you do need to memorize what cards have been folded that are relevant to your own requirements, and also what cards have been folded that are relevant to hands which may eventually beat yours.

9. EQUANIMITY. The Caterpillar, you may recall, gave Alice three words of advice: *Keep your Temper.* No one can hope to play Poker successfully who doesn't follow this injunction. A player who has lost his temper is certain to lose a great many chips as well, for other players will at once proceed to exploit advantageously the impairment of judgment which loss of temper implies. If you realise that your self-control is failing you, get out of the game as quickly as you can.

10. GOOD MANNERS. This is another adjunct to successful play. Try not to gloat when you win; to moan about your luck when you lose; to surrender a lost pot ungraciously; to resent unjustifiable criticisms of the way

that you have played. Good manners — as William of Wykeham reminded Winchester — are an asset in themselves; in a Poker game they're an asset which has a considerable cash value.

11. FLAIR. I feel bound to include flair in the list of qualities which make for success at Poker. But, though I know what I mean by flair, I can't define it with precision; if I could so define it, it wouldn't be flair. Let's just call it a sixth sense which you may or may not possess. Speaking for myself, I don't think I do possess it, and have to struggle on as best I can without it.

12. THE ABILITY TO KEEP ONE'S OPPONENTS GUESSING. Hardly any of the qualities I have listed transcends this in importance. (I would remind you of what, in Chapter XIV, Oswald Jacoby has to say). If you want to win at Poker, you must conform to a number of rules which can be stated with precision; yet perhaps the first of such rules is: *no rule is irrefragable*. Suppose, for example, that you're taking part in a round of Jackpots against players who all 'know' that you're not so silly as to draw to a small pair. Disconcert them, once in a blue moon, by coming in when you're not last to speak, and — if the opening bet hasn't been raised before the buy (in which case you quit) — drawing three cards to, say, a pair of sixes. If you make three sixes, you will probably win the pot; if you don't make three sixes, and are called on to show your hand, your money hasn't been wasted. You won't do the same thing again for a long time; but every draw you make to three cards is likely for some time to be suspect. An infinitude of similar situations could be listed; I dealt with some of them in Chapter XII.

THE CLIMATE OF OPINION

Let me now say something more about what I have called the 'climate of opinion'. If you are playing club Poker you will do well to bear in mind all the considerations which I have tried to bring to your notice. But you will also pay attention to conventions which — though they flout the rules which the winning player should follow — are tacitly accepted in your club. There are many clubs where 'sand-bagging' is frowned upon; it is considered bad form to check on a winning hand and subsequently to bet. If you are playing in one of these clubs, accept its convention and don't sandbag. You won't lose many chips by so doing; and it's far better anyway to lose a few chips than to lose your reputation for sportsmanship. If everyone at your table is playing a 'liberal' game, play a liberal game too — or, at any rate, play a game which has its moments of liberality. Get yourself known as a Rock of Gibraltar, and the only players who'll see your bets are players whose hands may well be better hands than yours.

In social games, privately organized, much of what I have said about club play is likely to go by the board. Betting may be on a very liberal scale; e.g., each successive bet may be half the rapidly-mounting total in the kitty. The tactics appropriate to club play will, in these circumstances, need considerable revision. My advice is to bet fairly freely as long as you hold what seems to be the best hand; in the long run that policy can't lose; but never, if you can help it, throw good money after bad. Let me here once again remind you that, once you've made a bet, the money you've staked isn't yours; it's the table's. You aren't defending your own property when you make another bet; you're venturing new money in exactly the same way as the other players are. There's no sillier resolution than that which I often hear uttered: 'Well; I must see it through'.

In these games, too, the etiquette rigidly enforced in clubs may go by the board altogether. 'Bluffing by word of mouth'. for example, may be recognised as part of the fun. Or players may take up, and examine, hands that have been thrown in; or, having thrown in, they may peer at their neighbours' hands, and suggest what discards they should make, or how many chips they should bet. Well; if that's what everyone else is doing, don't take offence, or behave like a spoilsport or a prig. In free-and-easy games of this type a good Poker player should be able to indulge in comparable antics and still get up a winner. And, if you don't care for games of this type, you are, presumably, a free agent; you can't be compelled to take part in them.

APPENDICES

APPENDIX A

GLOSSARY OF POKER TERMS

(Terms prefixed by an asterisk are of American provenance.)

A PRIORI ODDS. The odds against a particular event as determined by the application of the so-called 'Laws of Chance.'

ANTE. The small initial bet made in 'straight' Poker by the player to the dealer's left. The Ante (and Straddle) are put up before the cards are dealt.

*BACK TO BACK. In Five-Card Stud, a player who has, say, an Ace exposed and another Ace 'in the hole', is said to have 'Aces back to back.'

*BICYCLE. A hand in a Misère Pot (or, as the Americans call it, Lowball) which corresponds to our 'Royal', i.e. 6 4 3 2 A.

*BIG DOG. A ranking hand in some American games. There are four hands which are similar in type:

1. *Big Tiger (or Big Cat)*. Five cards, of which a King is the highest, and an 8 the lowest, and which do not include a pair; e.g., K Q 10 9 8.
2. *Little Tiger (or Little Cat)*. Five cards which, similarly, range from an 8 to a 3; e.g., 8 7 6 5 3.
3. *Big Dog*. The range is from Ace to 9; e.g., A Q J 10 9.
4. *Little Dog*. The range is from 7 to 2, e.g., 7 6 5 3 2.

   These hands rank among themselves in the order listed. Big Tiger comes next after a Flush, while Little Dog is superior to a Straight.

*BIG TIGER. See above.

BOBTAIL FLUSH. Four cards of a suit with one of another suit, e.g., = ♠ K 9 7 4 ◇ Q.

BONUS. A compulsory payment of an agreed number of chips to a player who holds a Royal Flush, Straight Flush, or Fours.

BUCK. A token which is put in the centre of the table when a pot is being played to indicate what type of pot it is.

*BUG. A Joker added to the pack for the purpose of some games (thus making it a 53-card pack). The Bug can be used as an additional Ace or to make up a Flush or Straight.

BURNT CARD. A card which has been misdealt and is consequently placed at the bottom of the pack by the dealer.

CHECK. To check is to make a bet of nothing; i.e., a player who 'checks' is still in the game but is not raising the amount already bet.

CHIP. (a) The 'chips' are, of course, the token currency with which, in clubs, the game is played.

(b) In some games the player who is first to speak is not permitted to check. He must make a bet of the smallest denomination permitted if he wishes to stay in the game. He will then say, not 'Check', but 'Chip.'

*DROP. To drop is to throw in one's hand.

*FOLD. To 'fold' one's cards in a Stud game is to turn them face downwards, signifying that one is not prepared to stay in the current deal.

*HOLE CARD. The unexposed card dealt to each player at the beginning of a Five-Card Stud game.

*IMMORTAL. In a Stud Game, a hand which its possessor knows is certain to win the pot.

INSIDE STRAIGHT. Four cards towards a Straight, of which at least one is higher, and at least one lower, than the card required if the Straight is to be filled; e.g., 10 9 7 6 and one other card.

*LITTLE DOG. See BIG DOG, above.

*LITTLE TIGER. See BIG DOG, above.

OPEN-ENDED STRAIGHT. Four cards in sequence, so that there are two chances of making a Straight, e.g., 7 6 5 4 and another card.

OPENERS. The cards which a player must hold before he opens a pot of a specified type. Thus to open an Acepot a player must have a pair of Aces or better. If he retires from the pot, he must retain his cards and show the hand that he opened on.

PENALTIES. The same as Bonuses (q.v.)

PENALTY POT. The pot which, in some clubs, follows the payment of penalties to one of the players.

*PIGEON. A card which—against all probability—gives one a winning hand in certain types of game.

POT. The term is used loosely to indicate all the chips that are being played for. In a stricter sense, a Pot is a deal where there is no Ante and Straddle, but all players contribute equally to the initial stake, their chips being placed in the centre of the table.

ROVER. A player who has been cut out of a table, or retires according to a rota, and is awaiting admission to another table.

REFRESHER or SWEETENER. A contribution from every player to a pot which has not been opened.

ROYAL or ROYAL SIX. A hand in a Misère Pot which cannot be beaten, i.e., 6 4 3 2 A.

SANDBAGGING. Lying low on a good hand, with a view to raising or re-raising bets made by subsequent players; or, when favourably placed, declining to open a pot although one has openers.

*STACK. In a Table Stakes game, the whole of the chips which one has in front of one.

STRADDLE. In 'Straight' Poker, the compulsory contribution by the player next but one to the dealer. It is generally twice the Ante (q.v.) and, like the Ante, must be put up before the deal.

SWEETENER. The same as REFRESHER (q.v.)

TABLE STAKES. A game in which each player starts with an agreed number of chips, and, during any particular deal, may not bet more than the chips he has in front of him. He can stay in any deal until the finish, but cannot win more than appertains to the maximum he is able to bet.

*TAP. To bet, in a Table Stakes game, the whole of the chips in front of one.

PRINCIPAL VARIATIONS IN PRACTICE
BETWEEN ONE CLUB AND ANOTHER

(A newcomer to a club should make quite certain, in every situation listed, what the practice of the club is.)

1. THE STAKES PLAYED FOR. The tyro should ascertain how much money each chip represents; what minimum bets (Ante, Straddle, etc.) are compulsory; and what maximum bets, at each stage of the betting, are permissible.

2. CHECK OR CHIP? Is the player who is first to speak after the buy permitted to check; or must he 'chip' (i.e., put up a chip of a specified value) if he wishes to remain in the game?

3. 'DO YOU WISH TO PLAY?' Is it permissible for the Ante to put this question to the Straddle if all players before the Ante have thrown their hands in?

4. POTS. (a) What contribution must each player make to the pot before the cards are dealt?

   (b) What sweetener is required when a pot has not been opened?

   (c) If a pot is not opened, does the original dealer deal again, or does the deal pass to the player to his left?

   (d) Is the amount required to open the pot increased after it has been sweetened?

   (e) If the opener of a pot has retired during the betting, must he subsequently show the whole of his hand, or will it suffice, if he only shows his openers?

   (f) 'Splitting' openers. Is this permissible? And, if so, must the opener announce that he is 'splitting', or may he do so without drawing attention to the fact?

5. FREAKPOTS. Do Fives rank above or below a Royal Flush?

6. BONUSES (or PENALTIES)
   (a) In respect of what hands are they payable, and what is the scale of chips applicable to them?
   (b) When penalties are claimed, does a 'Penalty Pot' follow?
7. CHOICEPOTS. On what occasions, if at all, are Choicepots played; and what range of choices is available?

APPENDIX C

POKER GAMES
NOT DISCUSSED IN THIS BOOK

THERE are literally hundreds of Poker games, and new ones are continually being invented. There would be no point in attempting to describe them all here, as few of them are played in our card clubs; indeed, I think I have covered all the varieties of the game that reputable card clubs play. But readers may be interested in the following, and wish to experiment with them in games played privately.

MEXICAN STUD or FLIP. The betting is as in Five-Card Stud, but all cards are dealt face down. After receiving his first two cards, and then after receiving each of the other cards dealt to him, each player decides which of his two unexposed cards he shall turn up.

HOKUM. A variety of Stud in which a player may turn up his hole card and ask for his next card to be dealt face down.

SPIT-IN-THE-OCEAN. A card is dealt face up in the centre of the table, and each player uses this as the fifth card in his hand, four being dealt to him in the usual way. Normally the centre card is a 'wild' card (i.e., the equivalent of a freak) and so are the other three cards of the same denomination.

CINCINNATI. Each player is dealt five cards face downwards and there are also dealt five cards face downwards in the centre of the table. These are exposed one at a time, a round of betting following each time a card is exposed. These cards belong to all players, who combine any of them they wish with cards in their own hand to form the best poker hand.

HIGH-LOW SEVEN CARD STUD. This is a complicated but exciting game, with a high skill factor; I expect it will presently be played over here.

The rules of Seven-Card stud apply, but the *highest hand* and the *lowest hand* divide the pot. Each player keeps the seven cards dealt him till the final betting round begins; then he selects five as his high hand and five as his low hand. (Obviously at least three cards must be in both of a player's selections.) It is possible, of course, for a player to win both high and low and hence take the whole pot — e.g., a player holding 6 4 3 2 A A A would at least divide the low pot with his Royal, and might well win the high pot with his three-Ace hand.

In one variation of the game a player must declare before the deal whether he is aiming at high, low, or both. If he has 'opted' for only one of them, his liability is, of course, proportionately limited.

THE LAWS OF POKER

*These laws are adapted (by permission) from those in force
at a well-known card club.*

INTRODUCTORY

1. The game of Poker is played by five, six, or seven players. Seven players form a complete table.

2. A single pack of fifty-two cards is used, containing four suits of equal value. The cards of a suit, except as stated otherwise in these rules, rank as follows: Ace (highest), King, Queen, Jack, Ten, Nine, Eight, Seven, Six, Five, Four, Three, Deuce (lowest).

3. Poker is played with counters which consist of chips, and half chips.

4. The game comprises plain Poker, and Pots.

THE DEAL

5. At the formation of a table the first dealer is the player occupying the lowest numbered seat. The deal passes in regular rotation to the left.

6. Every player has the right to shuffle the cards before the cut. The dealer has the right to shuffle last.

7. After the cards have been shuffled, the dealer hands the pack to the player on his right to cut.

8. The player entitled to cut may waive his right and run the cards. If he cuts the pack it must be divided into two packets each containing at least five cards.

9. If a card is exposed when cutting, the pack must be re-shuffled and again cut.

10. The cards must be dealt one at a time, face downwards in rotation from left to right, beginning at the dealer's left hand and continuing until each player has received five cards.

11. If a player deals out of turn he must be stopped before the last card is dealt, or the deal stands good.

12. If any card is exposed in dealing the player must accept the exposed card provided that it was not faced in the pack. If two cards are exposed in the same deal, whether dealt to the same or different players, there must be a fresh deal.

13. There must be a fresh deal if any card is found faced in the pack when dealing the original hands.

14. There must be a fresh deal if too many, or too few, hands are dealt.

15. If the right number of cards is off the pack at the conclusion of the deal, and there is a doubt about the particular cards any player is entitled to receive, the dealer may adjust the cards so that each player has his correct number of cards.

16. If at the conclusion of the deal one card too many is off the pack, the dealer may return this card to the top of the pack, and the deal stands good if otherwise in order. If more than one card too many is dealt, there must be a fresh deal.

17. If at the conclusion of the deal too few cards are off the pack and the dealer has not seen his hand, he may continue the deal if able to ensure that each player has his correct cards. Otherwise there must be a fresh deal.

18. If a player picks up the wrong hand he must hand it to the player entitled to receive it, and his own hand is dead, provided that the other player may, if he wishes, agree to accept the unseen hand before seeing either hand: in which case the exchange holds good.

19. If a player finds that he has more or less than the correct number of cards he may call attention to the fact before looking at his hand. If his neighbour also has the wrong number the dealer shall adjust.

20. If a player with the wrong number of cards has looked at his hand, his hand is dead, except as provided in Laws 22 and 23.

21. A player whose hand is dead may take no part in the play that deal, and forfeits any counters he may have put up, except that if his hand becomes dead before the draw, he may play on putting up the necessary stake and draw five fresh cards.

22. If a player has only four cards, and his neighbour, who has looked at his hand, has six cards, the hand of six cards is dead, but the dealer should choose one of the six cards at random and give it to the player with four cards.

23. If a player has six cards in front of him which he has not seen, and his neighbour has four cards which he has seen, the dealer must give the player with four cards one of the unseen cards to complete his hand.

PLAIN POKER

24. The player on the dealer's left is known as the first ante. He must make a contribution of one chip, known as the first ante or blind.

25. The player on the left of the first ante is known as the second ante. He must put up two chips, known as the second ante or straddle.

26. The amounts contributed before the deal by the first and second ante are compulsory. No other player may put up chips before the deal. There is no optional straddle.

27. The player on the left of the second ante must indicate that he will play or pass. If he passes he discards his hand. If he plays he must put up a stake.

28. If the first to speak throws in his hand his rights pass to the player on his left. If all the other players throw in their hands the second ante takes the chips on the table, and the deal passes.

29. When a player enters the game by putting up the necessary stake, the player on his left may enter by putting up the same stake, or may raise the stake, or may throw in his hand. If he throws in his hand his rights pass to the next player on his left, and so on round the table.

30. Any subsequent player entering the game may do so for the value of the stake already put up, or may raise the stake. If either ante takes part in the hand he adds counters to those in front of him so as to make up the necessary amount.

31. If a player speaks out of turn the player whose turn it was to speak is not deprived of his rights. So long as a player holds his cards and has not signified his intention to throw in, his rights remain.

32. A player who enters the game must put up the full stake. If he does so it is not necessary for him to speak, except as provided in Law 33.

33. A player must speak and announce his intention if he has previously put up a counter or counters, or if he puts up other than the exact amount, or if he is raising the stake.

34. A person who puts up more than the minimum amount is

assumed to be playing for the minimum unless he announces the contrary.

35. If the original stake has been raised, the player who put it up may abandon his hand, forfeiting the amount put up, or may make up his stake to the increased value, or may again raise the stake. Each player in turn has similar rights.

36. Betting before the draw ceases when all players have put up the amount necessary to compete, or have abandoned their hands.

37. A person who abandons his hand after having entered the game on account of a subsequent raise leaves his counters on the table and they become the property of the winner of the hand.

THE DRAW

38. When the betting before the draw is complete each of those still in the game is entitled to discard any or all of his cards and draw others in their places.

39. The dealer gives cards from the top of the pack, each player receiving the number of cards for which he asks in order starting on the dealer's left.

40. A player taking cards must ask distinctly for the number he wants, and discard that number from his original hand. When helping himself the dealer must state aloud the number he takes.

41. A player asking for cards may alter his request only if he does so in the same breath, or before the dealer has removed cards from the pack in response to his request.

42. A player must reply to a question as to how many cards he has drawn, provided that the question is put by a player still in the game and before the last card in the draw is given. The dealer must state at any time the number of cards he has drawn himself if questioned. Otherwise, no information may be given.

43. If any card is found faced in the pack when cards are given for the draw it must be placed amongst the discards after having been shown and named to all the players.

44. If one or more cards are exposed by the dealer when giving cards for the draw the player may not take the exposed card or cards, but must wait until all the other players, including the dealer, have been helped. He then receives a card or cards from the top of the pack in place of the exposed card or cards. The player retains any other cards given to him but not exposed.

45. A card is not deemed to have been exposed by the dealer if before it is faced it touches the player for whom it is intended,

whether given in the deal or in the draw. No card given by the dealer to himself is an exposed card.

46. If there is any doubt about the actual cards given to a player it is the duty of the dealer to decide. Players must abide by his decision.

47. In giving cards for the draw the dealer must not give the bottom card of the pack. If there are not sufficient cards to help everyone, then the bottom card and the cards already discarded by other players are mixed together by the dealer, who shuffles the pack so formed and hands it to the player on his right to cut. After it has been cut the dealer resumes giving cards for the draw.

48. A player demanding cards in the draw should at the same time discard the number he wants. If he omits to do so and cards are given in order and picked up by another player, he cannot subsequently object and must be assumed to have asked for the number actually given him.

49. A player who demands cards and at the same time discards is not penalized if the wrong number is given him, provided he points out the error before picking up the cards given. If, meanwhile, another player has picked up cards given in the draw, the adjustment must be made after the giving of cards to all the players in the game is complete, either by placing unseen in the discard the card or cards given in excess or by giving from the top of the pack a card or cards to make up the deficit.

AFTER THE DRAW

50. At plain poker the first player to speak after the draw is the player who first entered the hand. He may either check, signifying that he does not raise the stake, or he may raise the stake.

51. If the first player checks the others may also check, and there is a showdown, no further stake being put up.

52. Any player who raises the stake may do so in accordance with Law 91. He may double the amount of the stake already put up, provided that the amount of the raise does not exceed eight chips.

53. When a player does not wish to see a raised stake he abandons his hand, leaving in the pool all the counters that he has put up.

54. When a bet has been raised, any other player still in the game may call the bet by putting up the amount of the raised bet, or may again raise the bet.

55. When the last raised bet has been called, and there is no

further betting, there is a showdown. The pool is taken by the player with the hand which ranks highest.

56. The first to speak after the draw, if he checks or bets before picking up the cards given him in the draw, is entitled to the pool if the check or bet is not called, provided he was dealt the correct number of cards originally.

57. Except as provided in Law 56, the hand of a player with the wrong number of cards in the final showdown is dead.

58. In the showdown each person in the game must expose his hand face upwards on the table so that no card is touching any other card.

59. If there is any dispute about the value of a hand in the final showdown a person who has not exposed his hand as described in Law 58 is assumed to have been in the wrong.

THE RANK OF HANDS

60. Hands rank in the following order:

Royal Flush: Ace, King, Queen, Jack, Ten, of the same suit.

Straight Flush: Five cards of the same suit in sequence, not being a Royal Flush. The Ace ranks low.

Fours: Four of a kind and an odd card.

Full Hand: Three of a kind and a pair.

Flush: Five cards of the same suit, not being a Royal or Straight Flush.

Straight: Five cards in sequence, not being a Royal or Straight Flush. The Ace may rank high or low.

Threes: Three of a kind and two odd cards.

Two Pairs: Two pairs and an odd card.

One Pair: One pair and three odd cards.

No Pair: Hands not containing a pair or better.

61. When two or more hands of the same description meet, and are higher than any other hand, there is a tie if all five cards are of the same rank; otherwise the hand which ranks highest is as follows:

Straight Flushes and Straights: The hand with the highest card except that Five, Four, Three, Deuce, Ace, ranks lowest.

Fours: The hand with the highest fours.

Full Hand: The hand with the highest threes.

Flush: The hand with the highest card. If the highest card is the same, the hand with the next highest card, and so on.

Threes: The hand with the highest threes.

Two Pairs: The hand with the highest pair. If the highest pair is the same, the hand with the next highest pair. If both pairs are the same, the hand with the highest odd card.

One Pair: The hand with the highest pair. If two hands have the same highest pair, that with the highest odd card; if these are the same, the hand with the next highest; and so on.

Hands with Less than a Pair: The hand with the highest card. If the highest cards are the same, the hand with the next highest card; and so on.

JACKPOTS

62. When a jack pot is played every player contributes two chips, and the amount so subscribed forms a pot. There are no antes. The cards are dealt as in plain Poker.

63. The player on the left of the dealer is the first to speak. He may open the pot provided his hand is as good as a pair of Jacks, or better. If he decides not to open, each player in turn, beginning on his left, has the right to do so.

64. If no player opens the pot the pot is sweetened by every player contributing one half-chip. The deal then passes and each player in turn again has the right to open the pot.

65. On each occasion when the pot is not opened, a further sweetener of one half-chip is added to the pot.

66. After the pot has been opened every player starting on the left of the opener has the right to enter the pot, or to increase the opening stake. This includes players who have previously refused to open. The betting before the draw may then proceed as in plain Poker, subject to Law 91.

67. When all players taking part in the pot have put up the necessary stake, and the others have withdrawn, cards are given for the draw as in plain Poker.

68. The player who starts the betting after the draw is the opener. He may either check or raise the bid. The betting then proceeds as in plain Poker, subject to Law 91.

69. A player who opens a jackpot must not discard so as to split his opening qualification without announcing that fact. If he announced that he is splitting his openers he may draw as he likes, provided that he is able to establish that he possessed the necessary qualifications for opening. If he splits his opening qualification

without making such an announcement he is assumed not to have had openers.

70. The opener of a jackpot must expose his full hand after the pot has been won.

FALSE OPENERS

71. Should a player open without the proper qualification his hand is dead and all he has put into the pot is forfeited.

72. Should any player have come into play against the false opener, the pot shall be played for just as if it had been properly opened.

73. When a pot has been falsely opened and play proceeds, the pot is won by the hand of highest rank in the final showdown regardless of whether that hand could have opened the pot or not.

74. Where there is no competition against the opener in the final showdown, either because nobody else has entered the pot or because nobody has called the opener's check or bet, and it is found that the opener has not the necessary qualifications, the pot must be played for again. Any player may withdraw the amount he has put in subsequent to the pot being opened except the opener himself, who leaves in all he has contributed.

75. When there has to be a re-play in accordance with the last rule the opener is dealt out of the pot and may not take part in the game until the pot has been finally won.

76. There is no penalty for falsely opening a pot, except as provided above. The opener does not have to replace the pot.

FREAK POTS

77. A freak pot is played after the jackpot is finished. In a freak pot the four Deuces are known as freaks and are treated as Jokers.

78. Subject to Law 79, a player with one or more freaks in his hand may treat such freak or freaks as having the value of any card not in his hand, except that two freaks may not both represent the same card.

79. The value of hands rank as in plain Poker, but there is a new description of hand known as fives. This is held when the cards in the hand, other than freaks, are all of the same value.

80. A hand containing five ranks below a Royal Flush, but above a Straight Flush.

81. The laws for opening, sweetening, entering, and raising the

bid in freak pots are the same as for jackpots, except that no opening qualification of any kind is required.

82. In giving cards for the draw in a freak pot Law 47 does not apply. The dealer must give the bottom card of the pack.

83. If there are not enough cards to give any player the number he wants he may, if he wishes, abandon his hand and take back his entry chips.

MISÈRE POTS

84. A misère pot is dealt after a freak pot. The object is to get a hand which ranks lower in value than any other hand. Such a hand takes the pot on the final showdown.

85. The cards rank the same as in plain Poker, except that the ace is always considered to be the lowest card and never the highest.

86. If a card is exposed in dealing a misère pot, Law 12 does not apply. There must be a fresh deal, subject to Law 45.

87. In giving cards for the draw Law 39 is modified. No player may discard more than three cards.

88. The laws for opening, sweetening, entering, and raising the bid are the same as in jackpots, except that no opening qualification of any kind is required.

THE STAKE

89. The first player to speak at plain Poker may put up a stake of not less than four nor more than eight chips.

90. A player opening a pot must put up a stake of four chips.

91. A person raising a stake may do so by any sum from a half a chip up to the amount of the stake already put up, provided that in no case may he increase the stake by more than eight chips.

92. The amount contributed by a player before a pot is opened is not to be considered part of his stake.

93. The counters in front of a player must not be less than, and if possible should be exactly, the amount for which he is liable.

94. A player must not interfere with the counters of another player, nor take change from the pool. A player who disregards this rule is assumed to be in the wrong should any dispute occur.

SPEAKING OUT OF TURN

95. If a player out of turn speaks, or indicates otherwise that he will or will not call, raise, open a pot, or take part in the hand, his

speech or indication is cancelled. The right reverts to the proper player. When it comes to the turn of the offender he is subject to Laws 96 to 99.

96. If a player out of turn passes, abandons his hand, refuses to call a bet, or otherwise indicates that he withdraws, his hand becomes dead.

97. If a player out of turn refuses to open a pot he is debarred from opening when his turn comes, but he may compete if the pot is opened by another.

98. If a player out of turn makes a bet, when his turn comes:

(a) If no bet has been made meanwhile he must make the bet he made out of turn.
(b) If a smaller bet has been made he must raise to the extent of the bet made out of turn.
(c) If an equal bet has been made he must call.
(d) If a larger bet has been made he may call or raise, or he may withdraw on forfeiting an amount equal to the bet made out of turn.

99. If a player out of turn announces that he will play, or puts up a stake, or opens a pot, or calls, or raises a bet, Law 98 applies, so far as may be to the altered circumstances.

IMPERFECT PACK

100. If a pack of cards is discovered to be imperfect, the deal in the course of which the discovery is made is cancelled, and all stakes made in the course of the subsequent play are withdrawn. There must be a fresh deal by the same dealer. Previous play is not affected.

ETIQUETTE

There are certain breaches of the laws for which no penalties are imposed, partly because of the difficulty in enforcing them, and partly because the good sense of players should render such penalties unnecessary. There are also certain standards of play generally observed by club players, although not specifically laid down. The following may be mentioned:

It is a recognized principle of Poker that a player should not discuss the contents of his hand, or suggest by any statement or mannerisms whether it is good or bad. He has a free hand in the betting only.

A player who makes a mistake which he corrects in time, or makes any other breach of the rules, or makes any remark about his hand, should avoid raising the stake.

Disputes arising between players should be settled, if possible, by the players involved. If they arrive at an agreement no other player should interfere.

Players should not demand a ruling on a point of law unless it is essential for the continuance of the game.

In respect of a matter already finished, a player with a grievance may bring it before the Committee subsequently.

Players should recognize that it is not easy for most players to see an exposed hand unless it is spread out fully in the way required by Law 58.

Speech is not as a rule necessary, but where required it should be clear and without ambiguity.

Where there is a doubt about words used by a player his own statement about the words he used should be accepted.

The dealer should at all times be particularly alert. It is his business to control the game, and to be clear about all questions of fact.

It is of the utmost importance that no player should throw his cards out of turn. The effect of doing so, while it brings him no advantage, may radically alter the play of others, and operate unfairly to their disadvantage.

It is unfair knowingly to open a jackpot without the proper qualification. A player who does so inadvertently should announce his mistake as soon as he discovers it.

A player who is out of the game should not retain cards in his hand, unless he has opened a jackpot. The practice of doing so in other cases is apt to mislead players still in the game.

The dealer, when giving cards for the draw, should await the player's discard, so as to ensure giving the right number.

A player intending to play should do so as soon as a table is formed, and should not await the arrival of other players.

A player has full discretion to bet his cards as he likes and should never be criticized for betting or failing to bet.

MATHEMATICAL DATA

MATHEMATICS—as I have, I hope, made clear—are a good servant to the Poker player but a bad master. Other weapons in his armoury are just as important as mathematical knowledge; after the buy they become a great deal more important. But mathematical knowledge the equipped Poker player must have; or, if he doesn't have it, he must be exceptionally gifted in other ways to make up for his deficiency.

In this Appendix I propose to say something of the elementary principles which underlie the rules that good Poker players will normally follow when betting before the buy. These principles are based opon the so-called 'laws of chance' or 'laws of probability,' so far as they are relevant. The term 'law' is used here in the scientist's, not the jurist's, sense of the word: a 'law' is a generalized statement of what will hold good in the long run.

If you are not interested in these abstract propositions, there is no reason whatever why you should bother with this Appendix. It will add little of practical importance to what has been told you already. But I believe that a great many readers of this book will—like me—find the formulation of these 'laws of chance,' so far as they refer to Poker, interesting; moreover, there are a few situations in which a knowledge of them may well facilitate making a correct decision.

COMBINATIONS

Before we get around to the laws of chance, let me say something about a mathematical notion with which everyone who has ever studied elementary algebra must at some time have been familiar. This is the theory of *Combinations*. Combinations have reference to the number of ways in which a given number of things, events or abstractions, can be selected from a larger number. For example, if you have seven children and are sent three tickets for the circus, you can choose three out of the seven in 35 different ways. (If you don't believe this, call the children A, B, C, etc., and write down every selection of three of the letters A to G. You will find that there are 35 possible selections.)

The millions of people who play the football pools are very familiar with combinations in this sense. For the most part, what appeals to them in these gigantic lotteries is the possibility of guessing successfully that eight nominated matches will be drawn. And most of them have recourse to what, oddly, are called 'permutations'— oddly, because 'permutations' has reference to a different mathematical concept. The football tipster who first used the term had forgotten his algebra. A good many punters, I believe, nominate twelve matches from which every selection of eight matches constitutes a separate entry, and these punters don't need to be told by me that there are 495 of these selections (though they may not know how that number is arrived at).

The mathematical formula for a combination is normally written ^nC_m, where n represents the number you are selecting from, and m the number you wish to select. Thus the number of ways in which you can select three children from a total of seven is written $^7C_3$, and the number of ways in which eight football matches can be selected from twelve is written $^{12}C_8$.

Now why is $^7C_3$ equal to 35, and why is $^{12}C_8$ equal to 495? These answers are determined by a simple formula. Here it is:

$$^nC_m = \frac{n!}{m! \times (n-m)!}$$

I won't try to explain here how this formula is arrived at, or before I know where I am I shall be writing an introduction to elementary algebra. If you can't answer this question for yourself, ask any intelligent teenager to answer it for you.

Now combinations play a considerable part in Poker calculations. For example, the number of Poker hands that can be dealt from a 52-card pack is, as we know, 2,598,960. This number is $^{52}C_5$, i.e.,

$$\frac{52!}{5! \times 47!}$$

I had better explain what numbers followed by an exclamation mark mean. The exclamation mark is not intended to express

surprise or bewilderment; '$n!$' merely means all the numbers from
1 up to n multiplied together, i.e., $1 \times 2 \times 3 \times 4 \times 5 \ldots . n$.
So the formula ^nC_m, when one comes to work it out, always in-
volves, to begin with, the division of the number in the numerator
by the larger of the numbers in the denominator.

$$^{52}C_5 = \frac{52!}{5! \times 47!} = \frac{48.49.50.51.52}{1.2.3.4.5} = 2.49.10.51.52*$$

and this is equal (you can work it out in two minutes) to 2,598,960.

Ranking of Poker Hands

The ranking of Poker hands is based (as was mentioned in
Chapter II) on the relative chances of their being dealt 'pat'. But
how are these relative chances arrived at? If you know this, you
are, of course, no better equipped as a Poker player than you are if
you don't know it; so the explanation — which I now propose to
offer — is properly reserved for this Appendix.

But I am so often asked *why* there can be 5,000-odd Flushes
dealt pat, and 10,000-odd Straights; why there is roughly a 50–50
chance of being dealt a pair or better, and so on, that I am
confident that the answers to these and similar questions will be
read with a good deal of interest.

Let me then, to begin with, reproduce again the table showing
the composition of the 2,598,960 different hands which can be
dealt from a 52-card pack. This time it is given in more detail than
in Chapter II:

Royal Flushes	..	..	..	..	..	4
Straight Flushes (other than Royal Flushes)					..	36
Fours	..	..	..	..	..	624
Full Houses		..	..	..	..	3,744
Flushes	..	..	..	..	..	5,108
Straights	..	..	..	..	..	10,200
Threes	..	..	..	..	..	54,912
Two Pairs	..	..	..	..	..	123,552
One Pair	..	..	..	..	..	1,098,240

No Pair, Straight, or Flush:

Ace high ..	..	..	..	502,860
King high	..	..	..	335,580

*The dots in these expressions represent the multiplication sign.

Queen high	..	..	..	213,180
Knave high	..	..	..	127,500
Ten high..	..	..	..	70,380
Nine high	..	..	..	34,680
Eight high	..	..	..	14,280
Seven high	..	..	..	4,080
No Pair, etc.	..	..	..	.. TOTAL	1,302,540

GRAND TOTAL 2,598,960

How are the Figures Just Tabulated Arrived At?

(1) ROYAL FLUSHES

The question is very simply answered. There are four suits, and one Royal Flush in each suit. So the answer is 4.

(2) OTHER STRAIGHT FLUSHES

This is an equally simple problem. A Straight Flush (other than a Royal) may be headed by any of the nine denominations K Q J 10 9 8 7 6 5. Hence there are 9.4 = 36 Straight Flushes.

(3) FOURS

Fours can be held in any one of thirteen denominations, ranging from Ace to 2. And the fifth card may be any one of the remaining 48. So the number of Fours that can be dealt is 13.48 = 624.

(4) FULL HOUSES

Here we must apply our knowledge of *combinations*. A Full House consists of three cards of one denomination and two cards of another. So the two denominations can be selected in $^{13}C_2$ ways, i.e., $\frac{13.12}{2} = 78$. Now consider any one of these 78 selections, e.g., Aces and Kings. We can have either A A A K K or A A K K K. Three Aces can be selected from the four available in 4 different ways ($^4C_3$); two Kings can be selected in 6 different ways ($^4C_2$). Hence there are 4.6 different ways in which A A A K K can be selected, and another 24 ways in which A A K K K can be selected. Hence the total number of Full Houses that can be dealt is 78.2.24, i.e., 3,744.

(5) FLUSHES

This is another fairly simple calculation. There are four suits. A Flush consists of five cards of a suit. Hence the number of Flushes in each suit is $^{13}C_5$, i.e., 1,287. But 10 of these are Royal Flushes or Straight Flushes, and we have dealt with those already. So the total number of Flushes which have no higher rank is $4.1277 = 5,108$.

(6) STRAIGHTS

A Straight consists of five cards in sequence, headed by any one of the ten denominations A K Q . . . . . 5. And there are four cards of each denomination available. Hence the total number of Straights is 10.4.4.4.4.4, i.e., 10,240. But 40 of these are Royal Flushes or Straight Flushes; $10,240 - 40 = 10,200$.

(7) THREES

We need to make two separate calculations:

(a) How many selections are there of three cards of the same denomination? There are 13 denominations, and four cards of each to choose from. So there are $13.4 = 52$ possible threes.

(b) What of the two cards that accompany them? These must be cards of different denominations (otherwise we have a Full House). So our two denominations can be selected in $^{12}C_2 = 66$ ways, and there are 4 cards of each denomination available. Multiplying (a) by (b), we can have in all 52.66.4.4 hands containing Threes, i.e., 54,912.

(8) TWO PAIRS

Another fairly simple calculation. The denominations of our two pairs can be selected in $^{13}C_2 = 78$ different ways. There are 6 ways in which each pair can be selected from the 4 cards available ($^4C_2$). And there are 44 other cards, any one of which may complete the hand. Hence the number of Two Pair hands which can be dealt is $78.6.6.44 = 123,552$.

(9) ONE PAIR

There are 13 denominations to choose from, and four cards of each denomination available, each offering 6 possible pairs ($^4C_2$). The other three cards in the hand are of different denominations, so there are $^{12}C_3 = 220$ possibilities. And each of the three denominations offers four cards to choose from. Hence the total number of One Pair hands that can be dealt is $13.6.220.4.4.4 = 1,098,240$.

(10) HANDS CONTAINING NO FLUSH, STRAIGHT OR PAIR

(a) *Ace high.* This is a very tricky calculation.

We have in this hand one Ace and four other cards all of different denominations. $^{12}C_4$ is $495*$. But two out of these 495 selections don't count because they produce Straights (A K Q J 10 and 5 4 3 2 A). There are four cards of each denomination, hence we have $493.1,024$ possible hands.

But this number requires adjustment. We have eliminated Straights; we haven't eliminated Flushes. Each of our 493 selections includes four possible Flushes. Hence the number of Ace-high hands which don't include Flushes or Straights is $493.(1,024-4)$, i.e., $493.1,020 = 502,860$.

(b) *King High.* This calculation is on the same lines as the previous one, save that we have only $^{11}C_4$ selections to consider, since hands including Aces have been dealt with . $^{11}C_4$ is 330. And from this total one selection, not two, must be deducted, i.e., K Q J 10 9. This gives us 329 selections, to be multiplied, as before, by $(1,024-4)$, i.e., $1,020$. $329.1,020 = 335,580$.

No detailed explanation of the remaining hands should be necessary.

(c) *Queen high.* $^{10}C_4 = 210$; $(210-1) = 209$.
   $209.1,020 = 213,180$.
(d) *Jack high.* $^9C_4 = 126$; $(126-1) = 125$.
   $125.1,020 = 127,500$.
(e) *Ten high.* $^8C_4 = 70$; $(70-1) = 69$.
   $69.1,020 = 70,380$.
(f) *Nine high.* $^7C_4 = 35$; $(35-1) = 34$.
   $34.1,020 = 34,680$.
(g) *Eight high.* $^6C_4 = 15$; $(15-1) = 14$.
   $14.1,020 = 14,280$.
(h) *Seven high.* $^5C_4 = 5$; $(5-1) = 4$.
   $4.1,020 = 4,080$.

There can be no hand lower than 7-high, for a 6-high hand would necessarily be a Straight.

*The observant reader may have noticed that 495 is also $^{12}C_8$ (the Treble Chance selection of 8 matches from 12). So $^{12}C_8 = {}^{12}C_4$. Indeed, nC_m is always equal to $^nC_{(n-m)}$.

Calculation of Odds When Drawing to Four, Three, or Two Cards

Now let us turn to some simple problems which are of interest to Poker players and not only to those who take pleasure in mathematical calculations. On page 44 were given the odds relevant to various situations which it is important to memorize. How are these odds arrived at?

(1) DRAWING ONE CARD TO AN OPEN-ENDED STRAIGHT

This is the simplest of calculations. The odds against your filling your Straight have been given as approximately 5 to 1. This is near enough for all practical purposes. Actually the odds against you are 39 to 8. For suppose you hold 9 8 7 6. You need to draw either a 10 or a 5. You have five cards in your hand; you may draw any one of the remaining 47. Of these 47 cards, four are 10's and four are 5's. Hence 8 cards will give you your Straight; the other 39 won't. So the odds are 39 to 8 against you.

I may as well deal here with a point that puzzles many players. 'Your calculations,' they say to me, 'are based on the assumption that there are 47 cards available for you to draw from. But in fact this isn't true; six other hands have been dealt, so there are only 17 cards available. The card you want may not be among them at all'.

Very true. But if we examine our problem more closely, we shall find that my argument still holds good. We don't know which of the 47 cards not seen by us still remain at the dealer's disposal. It may be any selection of 17 cards from 47. If we took every one of these selections (a number so large that there would be no point in trying to work it out); calculated the odds against us in respect of each of them; and then totalled the several chances so arrived at, we should find that the result was precisely that reached by the simpler method of considering our 47 unknown cards *en bloc*. And this is equally true if we are drawing, not one card, but two or three or four.

(2) DRAWING ONE CARD TO A FLUSH

This is just as simple a calculation as the last one. We have, say, four Hearts in our hand plus one other card. We throw this card; what are the odds against our filling our Flush? For practical purposes, we assume that the odds are four to one against us. In fact they are not quite so good; they are 38 to 9 against us, or just under $4\frac{1}{4}$ to one. For of the 47 cards we know nothing about 9 are Hearts and the remaining 38 are no use to us.

(3) DRAWING ONE CARD TO AN OPEN-ENDED STRAIGHT FLUSH

This is an almost ideal draw. We hold, say, the J 10 9 8 of Diamonds. The ◇ Q or the ◇ 8 would give us a Straight Flush; any other Diamond would give us a Flush; any other Queen or eight would give us a Straight. So there are 9+6, i.e., 15 cards which will give us what is probably a winning hand, and the odds are only 32 to 15 (just over 2 to 1) against our getting one of the cards we want.

(4) DRAWING ONE CARD TO AN INSIDE STRAIGHT FLUSH

By an 'inside' Straight Flush I mean that you hold, say, the Q J 10 8 of a suit. Only the nine of this suit will give you a Straight Flush. But there are still other possibilities. There are eight other cards of the suit which will give you a Flush, and there are three other nines which will give you a Straight. So the odds against your making what is probably a winning hand are 35 to 12 (slightly better than 3 to 1).

(5) DRAWING ONE CARD TO TWO PAIRS

The only card which will improve a Two-Pair hand is a card of one of the two denominations held. If you hold, say, 10 10 6 6, either a 10 or a 6 will give you a Full House. There are two 10's and two 6's among the 47 cards you haven't seen, so the odds against your improving the hand are 43 to 4, i.e., $10\frac{3}{4}$ to one. (The odds are, similarly, $10\frac{3}{4}$ to 1 against you if you are making the draw—not normally justified—of one card to an 'inside' Straight; e.g., if you hold 9 8 7 5 (not of the same suit), only one of the four 6's will improve your hand.)

(6) DRAWING TWO CARDS WHERE YOU HAVE THREE OF A KIND

You can only improve Threes by drawing: (a) a Pair, giving you a Full House, or (b) the fourth card of the same denomination as your Threes, which would give you Fours. What are your chances of success?

This is rather a complex calculation. You are taking two cards, which means that you have to consider $^{47}C_2$, i.e., 1,081 possible draws. Suppose that you have started with Q Q Q 9 5. You will improve your hand if you draw: (i) the fourth Queen, together with any other card, or (ii) a Pair. You have 46 chances of drawing the fourth Queen plus one other card (i.e., the odds against your making Fours are $22\frac{1}{2}$ to one). You have three chances of drawing a pair of nines or a pair of fives, since there are only three 9's and three 5's available; and you have six chances ($^4C_2$) of drawing a pair of any one of ten denominations. This gives you 66 chances in all of making a Full House. Adding your two chances, the odds against your improving your Threes are 969 to 112, or $8\frac{2}{3}$ to one against you.

(7) DRAWING ONE CARD WHERE YOU HAVE THREE OF A KIND

This draw is only made for tactical reasons, e.g., where you have doubled the opener in a Jackpot and hope to get another double seen by giving the impression that you have originally doubled on two pairs. Your chances of improvement are easily calculated, and are obviously less than they would be when you draw two cards. Suppose you start with Q Q Q 9 5, throwing only the 5. Four cards will improve your hand: the fourth Queen or a 9. So the odds against improvement are (once again) $10\frac{3}{4}$ to 1.

(8) DRAWING THREE CARDS TO A PAIR

As this is the most frequent of all draws, we will explore it carefully. You hold, say, J J 8 5 3. You keep the Knaves and throw the other three cards. What are your chances of improvement

We have to consider $^{47}C_3$, i.e., 16,215 possibilities. You may draw (a) two more Knaves, giving you four Knaves; (b) one Knave and a pair, giving you a Full House; (c) three cards of the same denomination, also giving you a Full House; (d) one Knave and two other cards, giving you three Knaves; (e) a pair and one other card, giving you two pairs. Or, of course, (f) three worthless cards which don't improve your pair.

Readers (if any) who enjoy mathematical exercises, may like to try to analyse these 16,215 possible draws. (This would throw no light on their capacity to play Poker.) It's a somewhat intricate operation, though not in any sense difficult. As I couldn't lay my hands on the relevant figures, I have just worked the thing out afresh, and it took me about half an hour.

(a) Fours. This is simplicity itself. To get Fours, you must draw both the remaining Jacks, plus any one of the remaining 45 cards. So you have 45 chances in all.

(b) and *(c) Full Houses.* Let us consider the 47 unseen cards. There are two Jacks; three cards each of three denominations (8 5 3) and four cards each of the remaining nine denominations. I will call a card which is an 8, 5 or 3, *m*, and a card of the other nine denominations *n*.

Then to get a Full House we need:

(i) one J and two cards of the same denomination; or
(ii) three cards of the same denomination.

    (i) We can get one J and two cards of an *m* type; or one J and two cards of an *n* type.
    There are 3 denominations of type *m*, and three ways in which we can get two cards of each; there are 9 denominations, and 6 ways in which we can get two cards of each. So the number of possible Full Houses which include one J is $2(3.3+9.6) = 126$.

    (ii) We can get three cards of type *m*, or three cards of type *n*. There are only 3 cards available in each *m* denomination; there are 4 cards available in each *n* denomination, from which 4 selections of three cards are available; so the number of Full Houses here is $3+9.4=39$.
    Total of Full Houses available: $126+39=165$.

(d) Threes. We need to draw one J and two other cards which don't constitute a Pair. These can either be:

(i) two cards of type *m;*
(ii) one card of type *m* and one of type *n;*
(iii) two cards of type *n*.

Their respective chances are:

    (i) 3 denominations available, and 3 cards of each to choose from. $3.3.3 = 27$.
    (ii) 3 *m* denominations, and 9 *n* denominations, to select from. 3 cards in each case of type *m;* 4 cards in each case of type *n*. $3.3.9.4 = 324$.
    (iii) $^9C_2$, i.e., 36 selections to choose from, and 4 cards of each available. $36.4.4 = 576$.

So, since there are two Jacks, the chances of getting threes total 2 $(27+324+576) = 1,854$.

(e) *Two Pairs*. We can draw either:

    (i) one pair of type m and another card; or

    (ii)   ,,   ,, ,, ,, n ,,   ,,   ,,

        (i) There are 3 m denominations, and 3 ways of pairing the 3 cards in each; the fifth card can be any one of 42.

        (ii) There are 9 n denominations, and 6 ways of pairing the 4 cards in each; the fifth card can be any one of 41. $(3.3.42) + (9.6.41) = 2,592$; this represents our chances of getting Two Pairs.

(f) *No improvement*. We need either:

    (i) one card of each of the three m nominations; or

    (ii) one card of each of two m denominations, plus one card of an n denomination; or

    (iii) one card of an m denomination, plus one card of each of two n denominations; or

    (iv) one card of each of three n denominations.

The several chances are:

    (i) $3.3.3 = 27$
    (ii) $3.3.3.9.4 = 972$
    (iii) $3.3.36.4.4 = 5,184$
    (iv) $84.4.4.4 = 5,376$

      Total: $27+972+5,184+5,376 = 11,559$.

How the components of this total are arrived at should be apparent. 36 is of course $^9C_2$ and 84 is $^9C_3$.

Summary:

(a) Fours ..	..	..	..	..	45
(b) and (c) Full Houses ..		..	..	165
(d) Threes ..	..	..	..	..	1,854
(e) Two Pairs	..	..	..	..	2,592
(f) No improvement	..	..	..	11,559
			Total	..	16,215

From this somewhat alarming table, giving the precise *a priori* odds against the various chances resulting from a 3-card buy to J J, are deduced the rough-and-ready chances with which every player should be familiar. They are:

Against making Two Pairs or better   ..   .. $2\frac{1}{2}$ to one
   ,,   ,,   Aces up or better*   ..   ..   6 ,,   ,,
   ,,   ,,   Threes ..   ..   8 ,,   ,,
   ,,   ,,   a Full House   ..   ..   nearly 100 to one
   ,,   ,,   Fours ..   ..   ..   ,, 360 ,, ,,

(9) DRAWING TWO CARDS TO A SMALL PAIR AND AN ACE 'KICKER'

This draw is only important in one situation: where a player who has doubled the pot on two small pairs is re-doubled by the opener, and is therefore fairly certain that there are at least two better pairs than those which he holds against him. If he has an Ace in his hand, he stands a better chance of making up Aces (or a better hand) than he has if he draws to his two pairs.

Here, since we are drawing two cards, we have to analyse 1,081 ($^{47}C_2$) possible chances. Suppose we start with 8 8 2 2 A. We throw out the pair of 2's. The *a priori* analysis of our 1,081 chances works out as follows:

					Chances
Fours: we draw 8 8 ..	..	..	..		1
Full House: 8 A (6) or A A (3)		..	..		9
Threes: we draw 8 and another card ..			..		84
Aces up: we draw A and another card			..		126
Two Pairs (other than Aces up)			..		61
No improvement	..	..	..	..	800

Total ..   1,081

So now the odds relevant to this draw are:

	Drawing two cards	*Odds where 3 cards are drawn*
Against making:		
Two Pairs or better ..	Nearly 3 to one	$2\frac{1}{2}$ to one
Aces up, or better ..	4 ,, ,,	6 ,, ,,
Threes, or better ..	$10\frac{1}{2}$,, ,,	8 ,, ,,
Full House, or better ..	Over 100 ,, ,,	Nearly 100 ,, ,,
Fours	1,080 ,, ,,	360 ,, ,,

This shows that the only normal justification for this draw occurs in the situation summarized above.

*I have not shown how these odds are arrived at, but any reader who has understood the above can readily work them out for himself.

Drawing Cards in a Misère Pot

(i) ONE-CARD BUYS

Suppose you are buying one card to 9 6 2 A. (Not a very promising buy unless the pot lays good odds). What are the odds against your finishing with a 9-high hand?

It isn't a very difficult calculation. Any 8, 7, 5, 4 or 3 will give you a 9-high hand. Of the 47 cards not seen by you 20 belong to these five denominations, so the odds are 27 to 20—rather better than 3 to 2—against your finishing with a 9-high hand. Similarly there are 24 cards (four of each of six denominations) which will give at worst a 10-high hand; a (slightly better than) even-money chance. And if there are four or five other players in the pot, your 10-high stands a small chance of winning.

These are the *a priori* odds. But don't forget that, if there are a number of other players competing in the pot, the proportion of low cards left on the dealer's hand, and so available for the buy, is likely to be lower than the *a priori* odds assume.

And don't forget, either, that should you be buying to 9 7 6 5, your chance of winning isn't so good (apart altogether from the fact that 9 7 6 5 A isn't a promising hand to have at the finish). For an 8 would give you a straight, and so the *a priori* odds against your making a 9-high hand are not 27 to 20 but 31 to 16: roughly two to one.

Also if your four cards are all of the same suit the odds against your making an eligible 9-hand become 38 to 9: just over four to one.

Here is a table of approximate odds calculated on similar lines:

You are drawing to four cards not all of the same suit	Approximate odds against your making:		
	9-high or better	8-high or better	7-high or better	6-high or better
9 4 3 2	3 to 2	—	—	—
8 4 3 2	3 to 2	2 to one	—	—
8 7 6 4	2 to one	3 to one	—	—
7 4 3 2	3 to 2	2 to one	3 to one	—
7 6 4 3	2 to one	3 to one	5 to one	—
6 4 3 A	3 to 2	2 to one	3 to one	5 to one
6 4 3 2	2 to one	3 to one	5 to one	11 to one

To four cards
all of
the same suit

9 4 3 A	2 to one	—	—	—
8 4 3 A	2 to one	3 to one	—	—
7 4 3 A	2 to one	3 to one	5 to one	—
6 4 3 A	2 to one	3 to one	4 to one	7 to one

There is no need to memorize this table (though you might save a good deal of money by doing so). It is primarily designed to give you a general idea of your chances with a one-card buy, and to show how the odds against you lengthen if you are drawing to a flush or a straight. And if you are drawing to a Straight Flush the odds against you are still longer. Suppose, for example, that you draw to the 6 5 4 3 of a suit. The odds are 4 to 1 against your being 9-high and 7 to 1 against your being 8-high. There is obviously no chance of your being 7-high, and only one of three Aces will give you a 6-high hand: odds of nearly 15 to 1 against you.

(2) TWO-CARD BUYS

These, as I have tried to emphasize, are made far too frequently. I have already quoted Oswald Jacoby's advice (page 89).

To assess odds where you are buying two cards, you need (as we know already) to investigate $^{47}C_2$, i.e., 1,081 chances. For example, suppose you are buying two cards to 7 5 2. What are the *a priori* odds against your making a 7-high hand? You need two of the following cards: 6 4 3 A. So the relevant formula is $^4C_2 \cdot 4 \cdot 4$. Now $^4C_2$ is, as we know, 6; so the exact *a priori* odds against you are 995 to 96, or nearly $10\frac{1}{2}$ to 1. Here are some more useful examples of approximate odds similarly calculated:

You draw to 3 cards

not all of the same suit	Approximate odds against your making			
	8-high	7-high	6-high	'Royal'
7 4 A	6 to one	$10\frac{1}{2}$ to one	—	—
6 4 A	6 to one	$10\frac{1}{2}$ to one	22 to one	67 to one
7 5 3	$6\frac{1}{2}$ to one	$12\frac{1}{2}$ to one	—	—
6 4 2	$6\frac{1}{2}$ to one	$12\frac{1}{2}$ to one	33 to one	67 to one

If your three cards are all of the same suit, the odds against you are lengthened, but not to the same extent as where you are drawing to a Straight.

(3) THREE-CARD BUYS

These can only be worth while if one is last to speak and the pot lays unusually good odds. If, for example, it is a free type of game, and five people are already in the pot for 4 chips each, and if you are last to speak, the odds offered for your money are $8\frac{1}{2}$ to 1. You may—in optimistic mood—think it worth while to buy three cards to 6 A. The approximate *a priori* odds offered against your 3-card buy (calculated from the investigation of $^{47}C_3$, i.e., 16,215 possible chances) are:

Against your making a			9-high hand	..	.. $6\frac{1}{2}$ to one
,,	,,	,,	an 8-high ,,	..	.. $11\frac{1}{2}$,, ,,
,,	,,	,,	a 7-high ,,	..	..25 ,, ,,
,,	,,	,,	a 6-high ,,	..	..62 ,, ,,
,,	,,	,,	a Royal ,,	..	..250 ,, ,,

But don't forget that, with five players already in the pot, there won't normally be a fair proportion of low cards available among those which the dealer still has in hand.

I don't recommend a three-card buy in any circumstances whatever.

The 6 A holding which I have instanced is the best you can possibly have.

Notional Assessment of a Player's Chances of Winning in Various Hypothetical Situations

I remarked in the Addenda to Chapter VIII that the test of a player's prospects of success in a pot should be his expectation of a share in the 14 chips contributed before the deal. If he doesn't expect (in the mathematical sense) to take out of the pot some contribution—however small—towards the 2 chips he originally put in, he shouldn't play in the pot at all.

The notion persists, I find, among some players that because they have put 2 chips into a pot they are mathematically justified in risking another 4 or more chips because they are already committed to the modest outlay of 2. This is a fallacy. Once the chips are in the pot—and that's before the hands are dealt—they no longer represent individual stakes. The 2 chips paid are just a contribution to a total which is there to be competed for.

I propose now to explore a few typical or otherwise interesting situations in the light of the dictum given above.

(1) JACKPOTS

(*a*) *Drawing three cards to a small Pair.* Let us suppose that A (first to speak) has opened a Jackpot, putting up 4 chips. The next five players all throw in. G has a pair of 8's and elects to play. *This is the one situation in which play on a small pair is justified.* For any player, not last to speak, who enters the pot is liable to be doubled by a player who has not yet spoken. And, since it would be sheer madness to stay for the double, he will have thrown 4 chips away.

G (last to speak) is justified in playing on his pair of 8's, for the pot is offering odds of $4\frac{1}{2}$ to one, and the odds are only 4 to 1 against his beating the opener.

On these assumptions, he should win one pot in five. So in five pots A, the opener, will win four times, collecting 88 chips, of which 68 represents his profit. And G will win the fifth pot, collecting 22 chips, of which 2 represent his profit; i.e., the expectation of each of these players is, *vis-a-vis*, the 14 chips in the pot:

$$
\begin{array}{ll}
\text{A will win } 13 \cdot 6 \text{ chips} \\
\text{B } \quad,, \quad \quad ,, \quad \underline{\cdot 4} \quad ,, \\
\phantom{\text{B } ,, ,, } \overline{14 \cdot 0}
\end{array}
$$

This is, of course, a somewhat academic calculation, since it is based on the assumption that there will be no betting after the players have drawn cards.

(*b*) *Drawing one card to Two Pairs.* Let me, again, simplify this issue as much as possible. Suppose, as before, that A has opened the pot and that players B to F all throw in. G (last to speak) has two pairs (say 8's and 5's) and plays. There is no point in his doubling, as he might well do in any other position, to deter others from coming in. What are his *a priori* chances of success?

They depend, of course, on what A's holding is. There are, roughly, 63 chances in a hundred that he has one pair only; 23 chances in 100 that he has two pairs; and 14 chances in 100 that he has threes or better.

We can therefore (roughly) allocate 100 chances as follows:

	A	G
(i) G makes a Full House (4 chances in 47)		8
(ii) A, starting with a Pair, fails to improve.		
$\dfrac{58 \cdot 5}{7}$		41

(iii) A, starting with a Pair, improves   ..   17   —
(iv) A starts with two pairs   ..   .. $10\frac{1}{2}$ $10\frac{1}{2}$
(v) A starts with threes, or better   ..   13

$$40\frac{1}{2} \qquad 59\frac{1}{2}$$

It will be near enough, therefore, to assume that G, starting with two pairs, wins three pots out of five.

Hence, in five pots, A makes a profit of 24 chips; G makes a profit of 46 chips. Expectations concerning the 14 chips originally in the pot are: A: 4·8
                                                                      G: 9·2

$$14·0$$

(c) *Drawing one card to a Flush.* If A opens, and B is his only competitor, putting up 4 chips and drawing one card, the odds against him are, we know, roughly four to one, and the pot is laying him $4\frac{1}{2}$ to one—which justifies his playing. His expectation must be precisely the same as that of case (a) where one player comes in on a pair; i.e., we have as before: A: 13·6
                                                                                    B: ·4

$$14·0$$

But drawing one card to a Flush is otherwise a very different proposition from drawing three cards to a pair. The player drawing to a pair doesn't want competition, but the player drawing to a flush welcomes it. If no other player is also drawing to a flush, the one player who is doing so, and who makes his flush, is almost certain to win the pot. His mathematical expectation rises steadily as more players come in. If no player has raised the opener, the player drawing to a flush can expect to get the following shares of the chips originally contributed:

Where he has two opponents ..   ..   1·2 chips
    ,,   ,,   ,,   three   ,, ...   2·0   ,,
    ,,   ,,   ,,   four   ,, ...   2·8   ,,

and so on. These expectations are based on similar calculations to those already presented.

(d) *Drawing one card to an open-ended straight.* Here, as we know, the player making the draw is not on so good a wicket as is a player drawing to a flush. The odds against his success are roughly five to one, and therefore he should not play on his open-ended straight unless there are at least two other players against him. On the assumption that his straight, if he makes it, will win the pot, his expectation against two opponents is that he will win 0·3 of the 14 chips originally contributed; if there are three opponents, it rises to 1·0 chips; if there are four opponents, to 1·7 chips.

(2) MISÈRE POTS

Here it is quite pointless to attempt to investigate hypothetical cases where nothing is known about the cards that players may hold. The imponderable factors—to quote my favourite dictum—greatly outweigh such factors as are assessable. I have, however, thought it interesting, and perhaps useful, to consider three situations where the players' holdings, before the draw, are known.

(a) *A pat hand versus a one-card buy.* A, B, and C have passed. D opens on a poorish pat hand: 9 7 4 3 2. E and F pass. G doubles, holding 6 3 2 A A : the best one-card buy possible. D accepts the double, so there are 30 chips in all to play for before the buy.

D says, 'No cards'. G buys one. How do his chances of winning compare with G's? You would not be far wrong if you assessed the odds at 3 to 2 on D.

Let's work it out. There are 42 cards that we know nothing about. Their composition is:

> K Q J 10 8 5 4 each
> 9 7 6 4:   3 „
> 3 2 A: 2 „

G will win if, to his 6 3 2 A, he draws 9, 8, 7, 5 or 4.

There are 17 of these cards. So the precise odds against his winning are 25 to 17.

This doesn't mean, however, that G stands to collect 17·42 of the 14 chips originally in the pot. His double has worsened his chances. The expectations of the two players, *vis-à-vis* these 14 chips, are: D: 9·9 chips

> G: 4·1   „
> _____
>   14·0   „

If G had not doubled before the buy, his expectation would have been 4·9 of the 14 chips originally dealt.

(b) *Two promising one-card buys in opposition.* There are only two contestants for the pot: A, who opens on (K) 8 5 3 2, and F, who plays on a slightly more promising collection: (7) 7 6 4 A. What would you guess their respective chances of winning to be? If you assessed the odds at four to three on F, you'd be very near the mark.

And would it amuse you to see how the actual odds are assessed? It involves a lot of arithmetic, but it took me no more than a quarter of an hour to arrive at the answer.

There are 42 cards that we haven't seen. So we need to analyse 42 . 41 = 1,722 possibilities.

The cards available are:

Rank	K	Q	J	10	9	8	7	6	5	4	3	2	A	
Number of each:	3	4	4	4	4	3	2	3	3	3	3	3	3	Total: 42

Now if A draws	F to win must draw	A's chances	F's chances
K (3)	Any card except 7 6 4 A ..	33	90
Q (4)	Any card except K 7 6 4 A	56	108
J (4)	Any card except K Q 7 6 4 A	72	92
10 (4)	10 9 8 5 3 2	88	76
9 (4)	9 8 5 3 2	104	60
8 (3)	Any card: he must win ..	—	123
7 (2)	5 3 2	64	18
6 (3)	5 3 2	96	27
5 (3)	Any card except 7 or 6 ..	15	108
4 (3)	5 3 2	96	27
3 (3)	Any card excpet 7 6 4 ..	24	99
2 (3)	,, ,, ,, 7 6 4 ..	24	99
A (3)	5 3 2	96	27
	Totals ..	768	954

So the exact odds against A's winning are 954:768—rather less than four to three.

We now reach the final stage in this operation: to assess the two players' respective claims on the 14 chips originally in the pot.

They work out at: A: 5·8 chips

$$\begin{array}{r} \text{F: } 8\cdot2 \text{ ,,} \\ \hline 14\cdot0 \end{array}$$

Or, to put the thing another way, F will collect 22 chips (plus any bet after the buy) just about 4 times out of seven.

(*c*) *Four good hands in opposition to one another.* These hands actually occurred in a deal which I saw played, and I thought it would be interesting to work out the respective players' *a priori* chances of winning.

A, who opened, held 8 6 5 3 A

C held 7 6 5 4 2

D held (K) 7 3 2 A

G held (9) 4 3 2 A

Note that, of the 32 low cards in the pack (8 to A inclusive) 18 were included in the 20 cards dealt to these four players.

It is occurrences like these that vitiate theoretical speculations. A opened for 4 chips and, before the buy, no one raised him. C didn't want to drive out competitors; D doesn't believe in doubling on four cards only; G would have doubled normally on 6 3 2 A, but his 4 3 2 A isn't so hot: a 5 gives him a straight.

A, it will be noticed, has no chance whatever of winning the pot. C's hand has him beaten from the word Go. Tough luck, this, since he has, pat, a rather better hand than the average winning hand in Misère Pots!

So we are only concerned with C, D and G. Arithmetical calculations similar to those shown in the last example give the three players the following chances of finishing with the best hand:

C: 702 chances
D: 167   ,,
G: 123   ,,
───
992

$992 = 32 \cdot 31$: the number of draws by D and G which need to be considered.

And the four players' expectations *vis-à-vis* the 14 chips originally contributed to the pot work out at:

A: −4·0
C: +17·0
D: + 1·0
G: all square
───────
+18·0−4·0 = 14·0